THE TREASURE OF TENAKERTOM

Thurms, seventeen-year-old son of an Egyptian general, is banished from Thebes by his father for insubordination. Banishment means a tedious assignment of patrolling at the edge of the Sinai desert. But rather than a monotonous life, Thurms runs into adventure when he rescues Kemheb from Khabiri bandits. Kemheb, younger than Thurms, hints he is more than a runaway slave, as Thurms had supposed. His tale results in the pursuit of the treasure of the lost Tenakertom.

The TREASURE of TENAKERTOM

By Robert Edmond Alter

Illustrated by Frank Aloise

WILDSIDE PRESS

© 1964 by Robert Edmond Alter

All rights reserved

CONTENTS

	Genesis of a Legend	7
1.	The General's Son	9
2.	Make Bright the Blades of War	18
3.	A Line on Tenakertom	32
4.	Akhetaton	38
5.	A Croc For Kipa	51
6.	Gods Are Devious Creatures	63
7.	Fort Flea	73
8.	The Sands of Set	82
9.	The White Circle	97
10.	The Snake Pit	115
11.	Anar's Arch	129
12.	"Everything You've Ever Dreamed of Exists"	144
13.	The Gold Bug	155
14.	The Black Mouth	168
15.	Follow the Dark Star	183

TO HELEN JONES

> I saw a man pursuing the horizon;
> Round and round they sped.
> I was disturbed at this;
> I accosted the man.
> "It is futile," I said,
> "You can never—"
>
> "You lie!" he cried,
> and ran on.
> Stephen Crane

GENESIS OF A LEGEND

THREE THOUSAND YEARS before Christ, Egypt was divided into two kingdoms. The Upper Kingdom was in the south and it was known as the Nile Valley. It was ruled by an Egyptian king called Menes, a ruthlessly ambitious man with a politically sound dream. He wanted to unite the two lands, claim himself Pharaoh of all Egypt, and found the 1st Dynasty. With this goal in mind he led his armies, the Thinites, into the north and started a long and bloody war.

The Lower Kingdom was in the north and it was known as the Delta Land. Its principal people were the Wa-shi, who were still close enough to the barbaric state to wear wolf tails at the backs of their grass kilts and to tattoo their arms and legs, yet who were civilized enough to know how to build cities.

And one other thing they knew: Sinai—a desert and mountainous land to the east of them—was a treasure house. There were fabulous mines in the Umm Bugma Mountains of the Egma Plateau, and the Wa-shi meant to have these treasures.

Anar, a Wa-shi general, set out in 3000 B.C. to further the conquest of Sinai, striking for the distant mines of the Egma Plateau. Of Anar's success, little is known. Legend has it that he started northward on his homeward journey shortly before the fall of the Delta Land. It was in the Gebel Yelleq mountains that his expedition met a Wa-shi slave, a survivor of the Delta war, who told Anar that the Wa-shi colony had fallen to the Thinites.

Anar, with two thousand hard-bitten warriors, took a stand where he was and fortified a mountain pass.

Thus was born the city of Tenakertom, somewhere in the heart of Sinai. A city that waited for the Wa-shi survivors to fall back on her and form a new dynasty; that waited for the onslaught of Thinite legions.

That waited, and waited—until it became obscured and lost to the world, and became a legend for treasure hunters and soldiers of fortune and bright-eyed youths who dreamed pure dreams of lost cities.

1

THE GENERAL'S SON

It started out as any of the monotonous desert patrols. For Thurms, the General's son, it was his one hundred and fourth patrol along the frontier of the desert of Sinai.

It was the year 1356 B.C. and it was a time of peace for the great kingdom of Egypt. In the south the dark men of Kush were momentarily at ease, while far off in the northeast even the warlike Hittites were plucking olive branches to offer Pharaoh Akhnaton, as symbols of their devoted friendship. But in Syria and Sinai there were always the Khabiri—the barbaric desert marauders—and so there was no rest for Pharaoh's armies of occupation.

Thurms left the Daphnae barracks and walked disconsolately down a colonnade of palms toward the stables. He was seventeen years of age, had never seen a battle, and had been living in exile on the border of the Wilderness of Shur for five months.

He kicked at a pebble in his path, driving sharp little grains of sand between his toes, and muttered, "May Set and all his devils take this accursed land and swallow it in fire."

It was said of this 'accursed land' that every valley had its hill, and beyond each hill was another valley, and in each valley skulked a band of Khabiri that infiltrated from the desert every spring. It was a dangerous land and the Egyptian garrisons were hopelessly undermanned, while the desert patrols were merely a token defense.

But that was the manner in which Pharaoh conducted his government, because (1) Akhnaton was a thrifty man, and because (2) Akhnaton did not believe in physical force, and Thurms (who had been banished from Thebes until time of war, or until that time when he should prove himself valorous) was beginning to fear he would waste his youth in this flea-bitten land.

Hritut, Thurms' patrol companion, was standing by their two-horse war chariot awaiting him with impatience. Once he had been a young man of rank from an influential family in Thebes; now he too was in exile from the land of Kem. Cheating at dice and charges of numerous petty thefts had proved to be his downfall. A good boaster, Hritut, but a bad soldier.

"Will you drive, O favored one of the gods?" he asked Thurms, and his close-set unfriendly eyes were bright with mockery.

Thurms could never accustom himself to accept Hritut's barbed words indifferently, and early in their enmity had offered to fight him with swords. But Hritut had been wary of the thickness and reach of Thurms' muscular right arm and had refused with a sneer.

From that day on he had restricted his remarks to smirking innuendoes; and once, when Hritut had removed his sandals, Thurms noticed that the ne'er-do-well had painted an image of him in one of the soles—so that he might have the pleasure of tramping on the General's son at every step.

"No," Thurms said shortly. "I drove yesterday."

Hritut dropped to one knee in a mocking posture of deference, stretching an arm toward Thurms.

"Your desired wish is my law, valiant General's son," he said.

Thurms glowered and went to the chariot. It rankled him that their garrison commander, a taciturn embittered man called Bek, found some sort of perverse pleasure in uniting Thurms and Hritut on patrols—knowing full well that they couldn't abide the sight of one another.

That very morning Thurms had gone to Bek's quarters to see if something couldn't be done about the intolerable arrangement; only to discover, quickly, that he was wasting his time and breath.

Bek, a good soldier but a bad friend, a man without influential friends or relatives who had been shoved off on one flea-pestered desert post after another for the ten years of his military career, had little love for the son of a famous general who momentarily found himself at outs with his illustrious parent.

"You object to patrolling with Hritut?" Bek had snapped sourly.

"We don't like each other. We fight constantly. I thought that for the good of the service—"

"Suppose you let *me* worry about the good of the service," Bek had said impatiently. "I coupled the two of you together because you're both spoiled wastrels. That way I have both of you out of my hair at the same time."

"Yes, Commander, but—"

"Enough! General's son or not, Thurms, you're a long way from Thebes now, and you're under *my* command. I say you and Hritut will ride together until you either cut each other's throats or until the desert jackals get both of you. One way or another it won't matter much to me. Now get on with your patrol and stop wasting my time. And for once try to keep your eyes open. I've received a report that the Khabiri have become more aggressive than ever. The city of Katna has fallen to the savages and every Egyptian soldier was slain, as well as all the civilians—men, women and children."

Thurms was thunderstruck. Heretofore the Khabiri had been careful to avoid fortified towns when they started their annual depredations.

"Why, that sounds like the beginning of a full-scale war," he said. But Bek only scowled and made an impatient hand gesture.

"Perhaps so—in Syria. But this is Sinai, and there's no reason to suspect that we'll be troubled with anything more than a handful of marauders. However, a wary bird is one who does not allow himself to be caught off guard by the pouncing hawk. Now get on with your duty—you and your fine friend."

Thurms and his 'fine friend' Hritut approached their war chariot. The vehicle was of light construction, the coach being a basket weave and open at the rear. The driving or fighting platform was set on a long axle that supported the large, springy wheels, making the chariot maneuverable over almost any form of terrain.

Lashed to the sides of the basket were leather cases containing javelins, arrows and bows, and the two great double-edged copper blades which could be affixed to the wheels during combat—and which struck terror into the hearts of enemy foot soldiers. When a war chariot was in full motion and the wheels were spinning, those whirling blades could chop off the legs of an infantryman.

The horses were a sturdy matched team with ostrich

feathers stuck in their polls and dressed in thick leather pads to ward off enemy missiles.

Everything was ready and Thurms nodded at Hritut and stepped aside. Hritut, the corners of his mouth turning up like a crocodile's grin, climbed onto the platform and placed the looped reins around his hips. The team had been trained to respond to this method of hip-driving so that the charioteer's hands remained free to fire arrows if necessary.

Thurms stepped up behind Hritut. Custom was that he should ride with his arms about the charioteer's waist, but he would have none of this. He stood to one side clutching the javelin case, giving the platform a slight unbalance.

Hritut cracked the whip and the chariot bolted forward, careening wildly over rocks and stones. Hritut, Thurms reflected moodily, found a perverted sense of excitement in driving like a madman. The garrison and the southern fringe of the avidly green delta fell far behind in their dust-churned wake.

The sun, swollen with heat, radiated fixed spears of brilliant light, giving the sky the shimmering look of tinted glass. The chariot came banging down through the dark rolling hills and out onto the flatlands of the Wilderness of Shur, heading for the far-off Azira's Well, which was their turning point. Two or three miles across the plains the purple hills picked up again and ran with them like a distant endless battlement.

They saw little of interest during the long dry morning, except a filthy old sheepherder and his dark-skinned shy-eyed daughter. These they stopped to question about the Khabiri, but learned nothing.

Hritut jokingly attempted to intimidate the frightened girl, while her fearful parent stood by rending his clothes, indicative of his helpfulness in the hands of the Egyptian soldiers.

Thurms ordered the charioteer to desist, and Hritut threw up his hands in mock despair, wailing:

"I have made the General's son displeased. May the gods have pity on my ignorance and not turn me to stone!"

The sheepherder and his daughter didn't know what to make of this byplay and hung their heads in confused embarrassment. Thurms scowled furiously and leaped into the chariot, taking the reins himself. Hritut, grinning, winked at the girl and jumped up behind him, taking him about the waist.

The patrol continued in moody silence.

They reached the deserted and ageless well in the early noon. They watered the team, checked their hoofs, then sat in the palm shade to have their meal. They had nothing to say to each other until Hritut suddenly pointed toward the northeast hills.

"Look."

Thurms turned and saw a thin wavering band of blue smoke standing up from the hills, and he sighed, knowing that now they must go out of their way to investigate. But Hritut was in his usual slothful mood.

"Why not pretend," he suggested, "that Pharaoh's new sun god Aton entered our eyes, blinding us to the knowledge of the smoke? What you don't see you don't have to investigate—or report."

Thurms stood up to slap the dust from his tunic. "You would do well not to mock Pharaoh's god," he advised indifferently. "It profits you nothing. Come along. It's our duty to investigate."

Hritut placed his hands together in a mock supplication of thanks.

"Ah, the joy of working with a true warrior. Surely the gods have blessed me in this forsaken land!"

Thurms, as usual, said nothing.

They had to travel through a barren and hilly terrain, down a wide and very long rock defile to reach their objective. The chariot clattered out of the pass and onto a small bowl-shaped desert. Five miles across the flatland the rockheap picked up again and formed a ragged horizon going on around. A sparse and woebegone-looking oasis stood in the shimmering heat, nearly in the center of the desert.

The chariot rolled over the plain and into the palm grove. Thurms and Hritut dismounted, Hritut drawing his sword. A fat bearded man with oiled face and brightly wary eyes approached hurriedly, wearing the dress of a Syrian merchant. He prostrated himself before them.

"Welcome, mighty warriors from the land of Kem!" he cried, and he brushed the sand before their feet with his beard. "Wel—" He paused, spat sand, then raised his hands in delight. "Welcome!"

Thurms was embarrassed. He didn't like people to throw themselves on the ground before him. He turned away to look over the camp. The fat one's servants, or slaves—who looked suspiciously like Khabiri marauders—were standing in a sullen clump near the fire with their hands fussing inside their ragged garments as though in preparation for drawing knives.

Three shabby pack donkeys were browsing around a pile of jars and plump sacks, and a tent with the dreary aspect of a storm-wracked sail stood at the edge of the oasis. There was nothing else except the ruined wreck of an old war chariot, the sun-bleached bones of the horses still encased in their thick leather pads.

The fat one struggled to his feet, saying, "I am a poor

and humble merchant traveling from Gaza to trade with the desert people."

"Are you?" Thurms wondered, and he strode over to the pile of trade goods. There was an air of desperate geniality about the fat man that Thurms didn't trust. He knew he didn't have to worry about the Khabiri-looking servants, though: Hritut was very capable in dealing with matters of that sort. Without looking around he heard the charioteer harassing the sullen men.

"Bring your hands into the open, carrion-eaters. Let them dance in the air without the rib-ticklers I know are concealed in your lice-ridden tunics."

The fat merchant hurried along at Thurms' elbow, inviting him to look, to inspect whatever he desired. Thurms looked at the trade items: jars of oil and myrrh and sacks of onions. Then he wanted to look in the tent. Miraculously the fat one was suddenly in his path, bowing, smiling, clutching his tubby girth.

"The tent is for my children, illustrious warrior. A thousand pardons but it is not seemly for you to enter there."

Thurms placed his hands akimbo. "I'm not going to hurt them," he said impatiently. "I merely wish to look. Stand aside."

The fat one made a hurried, obsequious movement, yet somehow managed to end up still blocking the way.

"Ammon have pity on me if I appear disrespectful, but I must—"

Thurms stepped back, drew his sword and placed its point in the center of the man's expansive stomach. "Aside," he said simply.

The fat one blinked at the bronze blade, glanced surreptitiously at his servants, and then threw up his hands in dismay. He began rending his garments and pulling his beard, crying:

"It is not seemly! I protest! I—" But he waddled aside.

Thurms went to the tent and looked in. The merchant's 'children' was only one boy—a youth of sixteen with hair as black as the raven's wing and eyes that glittered like the green Nile water where it flowed by the spring reeds. A gag was tied about his mouth and his hands were lashed in the small of his back. He stared up at Thurms without fear.

2

MAKE BRIGHT THE BLADES OF WAR

THURMS LOOKED BACK at the merchant, who was now pouring sand in his hair to proclaim the extent of his despair, and said, "You lied to me. A man does not treat his son in this fashion."

"A thousand deaths from the teeth of the wolf of Asyut if I did!" the fat one cried. "I did not say he was my son—he is my slave. I purchased him from the desert tribesmen in good faith. I have the clay tablet to certify the transaction!"

Thurms squatted and removed the gag from the youth's mouth. Then, as the youth rubbed his lips and muttered something uncomplimentary about the merchant's rotund person, Thurms severed the bonds on his wrists.

"He lies," the youth said suddenly, and his eyes were like green dagger blades as he glared at the quaking merchant. "He kidnaped me from Tanis. His name is Azmachis and he is a Khabiri chief. He drew up the clay tablet himself to deceive foolish patrol soldiers. I am called Kemheb."

"Lies! Lies!" Azmachis wailed, and he began to enact a heart-rending scene—tearing his clothes, snatching his beard, hitting himself . . . "I bought him in good faith! The tablet is valid!"

Thurms said nothing. He was wondering if the youth meant that *he* was a foolish patrol soldier. He led him from the tent and ordered Azmachis to stop making a fool of himself. Then he turned to Kemheb.

"Whoever heard of a slave bringing enough ransom for a kidnaper to bother over?" he said.

Kemheb became quite haughty. "You should learn to look beneath the surface of things, soldier. There is more value to me than you dream of."

Thurms frankly doubted it; and besides that he found Kemheb's aloof manner annoying. "You act too proud for a common slave," he said admonishingly.

"And you for a common desert soldier," Kemheb snapped back.

"I'm a general's son," Thurms said in automatic defense, and he was irritated when Kemheb put a hand to his mouth to scoff behind.

Suddenly Azmachis began to speak in the Syrian tongue, a language that invariably left Thurms at a total loss. He did catch one word, however, that had a vaguely familiar ring to it: *Tenakertom*. Kemheb started to fire an angry string of Syrian words right back at Azmachis, but Thurms put a stop to it.

He was beginning to lose patience with Azmachis and Kemheb; nor did it help his temper to see Hritut coming toward them with his smirking grin. The charioteer roughly gripped Kemheb's arm in his hand, running his mean eyes over the boy's ragged Khabiri tunic.

"By Horus," he said, "this sprat isn't worth arguing over."

Kemheb showed fire. "Keep your hands off. I'm not your property, you carrion beetle!"

"He's mine! He's my property!" Azmachis cried.

Thurms looked at Hritut. "Take your hand from him," he ordered, and—as he'd expected—Hritut sneered.

"Fighting slaves' battles now, Thurms?"

"Remove your hand," Thurms repeated. He raised the tip of his bronze-bladed sword.

Hritut hesitated, then, grinning, let Kemheb go. But the last word was his. "He really is a general's son," he told Kemheb. "Isn't it apparent from his imperial manner?"

Thurms felt that the entire situation left much to be desired—from his standpoint. It was quite possible that Kemheb was nothing more than a slave; but if the youth *should* be a kidnap victim it was Thurms' duty to protect him. He turned to Azmachis.

"Bring me your tablet. I am taking it and Kemheb back to our garrison to determine the validity of your stories. You may follow on your donkeys if you desire."

Azmachis made a spectacle of his despair. He tore the clothes from his flabby chest, ripped clots of beard from his chin, and ran to the fire to find ashes to scatter in his hair. He called on Ammon to witness how he was being robbed of his rightful property. He called on Set to deliver a curse on all Egyptian soldiers who wouldn't heed an honest merchant's story . . . and, in the end, he gave Thurms the tablet.

Kemheb, still laughing at Azmachis' melodramatic antics, followed the two soldiers to the chariot. Thurms had to say this in the youth's favor: for a thin sixteen-year-old, who was either a slave or a kidnap victim, he was a nervy devil.

Hritut looped the reins about his hips, and Thurms and Kemheb stood on either side of the platform. Thurms noticed that one of the Khabiri-looking servants and one of the donkeys were missing from the camp, and he wondered just when they had slipped away and why.

The whip cracked, the metal felloes on the wheels clattered, and the chariot rattled into the desert.

"You were a fool not to take Azmachis in custody!" Kemheb shouted at Thurms above the quiet thunder of the chariot and team. "He cannot afford to let you take me back to your garrison. He knows the Egyptians will send a squadron of chariots after him."

Hritut laughed over his shoulder. "I should like to see that fat swine and his handful of jackals try to stop us!"

Kemheb pointed toward the approaching hills.

"The rocks are alive with Khabiri. They are Azmachis' tribesmen."

For an unhappy moment Thurms remembered the servant who had slipped from the oasis unobserved, and he considered ordering Hritut to turn about that they might return and take Azmachis into custody. But he couldn't bring himself to give the command. He was a general's son, and it wouldn't be fitting to admit that a young civilian's military judgment was better than his own. After all, he had no proof that Azmachis had not told the truth, and if Kemheb was a slave he was certainly nothing to start a desert war over.

He kept his mouth closed and watched the hills hurry toward them.

The chariot veered into the rock defile and went thundering down the pass. Hritut raised an arm in an ironic salute.

"Hail the triumphant coming of the General's son!" he shouted at the mute rock slabs. "Returning from the fields of glory bearing ragged slave boys and sacred tablets!" And he started to laugh.

An arrow went *bzzz-wit!* in the air, seemingly springing

from nowhere, ending its abrupt flight in the charioteer's left arm. Hritut made a startled cry, his hands flying straight up, and he fell back dragging the reins with the momentum of his body. The horses reared into a swerving halt as the air went *bzzz-wit, bzzz-wit* around Thurms' ears.

He crouched, grappling with Hritut's legs, trying to untangle the reins. Hritut was down on the platform, half-hanging over the edge, moaning, doing nothing to help.

"The reins!" Thurms shouted at Kemheb. "Untangle his legs!"

Miraculously the reins came free of the twisted legs and Thurms rose with them in his hand. The team bolted forward and Kemheb shouted. Thurms looked around wildly.

He was appalled at what he saw ahead. The floor of the pass and the sloping rock sides were crowded with ragged, bearded, howling Khabiri. Their shields and the tips of their spears sparked in the sun, and abruptly a dark flight of arrows whistled toward the chariot—*swisss-sss-sh!* Thurms veered the team left, then began backing frantically to come around.

Arrows went *tunk-tunk-tunk* against the chariot, against the leather cases and the jackets on the horses.

"Down!" Thurms shouted. *"Get down!"* But it was a needless order; the rocking, lurching motion of the turning vehicle spilled Kemheb into a disheveled clump of bare legs and whipping black hair on top of Hritut.

The turn was completed and they were charging full tilt down the pass and back toward the desert.

"They're not shooting at *me!*" Kemheb shouted from the vicinity of Thurms' braced feet. "It's you they want. I told you I was valuable!"

"That's something an arrow knows nothing about!" Thurms replied distractedly. He looped the reins over his hips and drew a bow, opened the quiver of arrows and began firing back at the Khabiri-clad slopes as they flashed along the alley. The heavy compound bow could drive the bronze-tipped arrows through a thick sheet of metal and what he hit stayed hit.

The chariot burst from the pass and charged the open desert. Thurms looked back at their wake and then replaced the bow in its case. No one was coming after them. He guided the team straight to the oasis.

Azmachis and his men were gone, but he had expected that. He skidded the chariot to a halt under the palms and leaped to the sand.

"Gather dates!" he ordered. Kemheb looked bewildered.

"Gather dates? Why, in the name of Ammon?"

Thurms ignored the question for the moment. He ran to Azmachis' abandoned trade goods and picked up a sack of onions and a jar of wine and trotted back to the chariot with them.

"We must fortify ourselves somewhere until we can figure a way out of this fix." He paused and looked around at the deserted plain.

"There must be a reason why they haven't pressed after us. I fear it is because they know the pass is the only way out."

He pointed toward the distant rock heap to the north of them.

"We will fortify ourselves in there for the night."

In the sand of the oasis pool he found a leather bucket, filled it with water, placed it in the chariot beside Hritut, and covered it with the sack of onions. He told Kemheb to watch that the bucket did not overturn as it was for the horses.

"How are you, Hritut?" he asked finally. "I'll take care of your wound as soon as I can."

"We're lost!" Hritut wailed. "We're as good as dead this moment!"

Thurms didn't see any sense in arguing about it. Hritut was a great boaster when he held the upperhand, but a hopeless pessimist when things went wrong.

In the hush of twilight they clattered once again across the desert.

The fort he selected was the crown of a barren hill partially surrounded by great rocks that stood up like pedestals of vanished statues; and it was Set's own work trying to bring the chariot and team into the shelter.

Kemheb watered the team and turned them loose to find grass, while Thurms went to work on Hritut's arm. The wound was not serious but Hritut did a great deal of shouting and cursing as Thurms removed the arrow and bound the puncture with strips from his tunic.

"Be happy it wasn't your neck," he advised Hritut.

"It might as well have been. We'll never get out of here alive. And it's your fault for bothering over that accursed slave boy!"

Kemheb had laid out their meager meal and Thurms fetched the water bucket and offered him a drink. Kemheb made a face and said, "Drink after the horses? What sort of swine do you think I am?"

"Well," Thurms said, annoyed, "a soldier looks upon his team as comrades in arms."

"Because you have so much in common perhaps," Kemheb said, grinning.

Thurms decided to stand on his dignity and allow the remark to pass beneath him. He ate his onions and dates moodily.

Night crowded over them and the stars were brilliant bits of splintered ice, while the moon hung like a golden falchion blade on a black wall. Kemheb studied Thurms' silent silhouette speculatively.

"Why," he asked finally, "if you are a general's son, are you patrolling the desert of Sinai?"

Thurms replied that he had been banished by his father for insubordination. "I was foolhardy enough to object to the time-honored military tradition of amputating the hands of the vanquished enemy while in the fury of combat."

Kemheb held his hands upright to express horror. "A most squeamish custom, surely," he said.

"Squeamishness had nothing to do with it," Thurms said. "I was merely trying to innovate a safety precaution. If a soldier stops to amputate a dead man's hand he is lowering his guard and becomes subject to a spear in the back. But when I persisted in belaboring my point my father, the General, became unreasonably wroth with me and called me a willful destroyer of sacred tradition, and banished me to this Set-cursed land until I could learn to think like a soldier."

"I am glad," Kemheb said, "that you had the strength of your own conviction." But Thurms shrugged and spoke bitterly.

"Yes—behold the good it has done me."

He dug a shallow slit trench for Kemheb and Hritut to sleep in, to give them a measure of protection from the desert night wind, then he went to the chariot for a quiver of arrows and a bow.

"Where will you sleep?" Kemheb wondered.

"I shall not be sleeping. I'll remain on guard for the night."

"Truly, you are a general's son."

Thurms had an uneasy feeling that Kemheb was grinning at him in the dark. He tramped off without a word.

The morning found him standing on the highest slab of

rock, staring down at the desert fixedly. From the distant movements of dust he realized that a few of the Khabiri were approaching the oasis, and his soldier's curiosity was whetted. He returned to the hollow and began hitching up the team.

"Gather our belongings," he ordered Kemheb. "We are going down to the oasis as soon as the Khabiri leave."

Kemheb sat up and looked around sleepily. "Where is Hritut?"

Thurms had dreaded the question, which he knew was bound to come, and he looked shamefaced. "I fear I dozed off last night while on guard," he confessed. "Hritut must have sneaked away. The fool. He will never escape these hills on foot."

Kemheb seemed unconcerned. "It's just as well. We don't need him."

Thurms nodded silently. It was certainly no place for cowards.

The marauders had retired to their secure hills when the chariot rolled into the quiet oasis. Only a crow greeted them, swooping off for the hills, tearing the fabric of the ovenlike air with its strident *kaw-kaw!* Thurms left the platform and walked through the palms, wondering what had brought the Khabiri back to the oasis.

He found the reason at the old wrecked war chariot. It was a clay tablet propped against the skull of one of the long dead horses. It was from Azmachis and it read:

> Greetings, General's son! Know that a prisoner may die slowly and with much unseemly screaming, or he may go free with honor and dignity. Will you come to terms regarding the slave?

"A gentle warning from the fat one," Thurms told Kemheb. "He's offering me freedom if I hand you over to him."

Kemheb gave him a level look. "What will you do?"

Thurms broke the tablet over his knee. "That," he said simply.

He looked toward the hills. Dust was undulating again before the mouth of the pass. It probably meant that the Khabiri were massing for an attack. And so . . . He looked at the wrecked chariot, at the dead horses, remembering the crow that had flown toward the hills—which might have been an omen—and made a decision.

"Remove everything from our chariot," he told Kemheb, "except the arrows and the bows."

He went to work on the skeletal horses, quickly stripping them of their heavy leather jackets. This form of protection had a circular opening for the horse's head and neck, and it covered the breast, flanks, and complete back from withers to dock in one piece. He dragged the jackets over to his own chariot and mounted them inside the coach, standing them up on end on either side of the platform, and lashed them to the basket-weave with their own harness.

"We will test the temper of the gods no further," he said. "We are going to run the pass."

He drew the long double-edged copper blades from their case and fitted one to each axle-hub. Then he told Kemheb to get in and sit on the platform. But the youth paused, looking at him.

"Will you offer sacrifice to Ammon for a safe passage, or do you prefer Aton?" he asked Thurms.

It was the custom, but Thurms had many private reservations about it. He did not consider himself a godless man but in his opinion Egypt had far too many gods. It was like a grab bag—to reach in and snatch when you needed one. Ammon, the most popular god of Egypt, he didn't trust at all. As a general's son he knew that the high priests of Ammon were nothing more than a pack of sacrilegious magicians and rogues; and Aton was a new god recently introduced by Pharaoh, and Thurms had not yet made up his mind about this mysterious innovation.

"Neither. I am a soldier and perhaps a skeptic. I place my trust in my horses, in my chariot and weapons."

Kemheb nodded understandingly. "And I place mine in you, Thurms."

The compliment embarrassed Thurms and he hesitated. Now that death was so near he found it quite easy to be honest.

"It is a soldier's duty to protect all Egyptians," he said, "slaves or not. But I would prefer that you and I did this as friends."

Kemheb grinned and held out his hand. "Comrades in arms, Thurms!"

Thurms smiled back and met his clasp. Kemheb was studying him with a wistfully serious look.

"Thurms, do you know that this is the first time I've seen you smile? I suspect that you've not had much pleasure from life."

"Perhaps not," Thurms said reflectively. "Ever since I was old enough to walk I've been trained for the military."

Kemheb slapped him on the shoulder. "Well, now that you've learned how to smile—see that you keep it up!"

Thurms followed him into the chariot and took his place on the platform with the reins about his hips. He retained his smile until he saw the dark and distant formation of the Khabiri coming from the hills. They appeared to be two or three hundred strong.

The oasis grew vague in their dust wake and diminished as though it meant to shrink to a pinpoint and vanish from the face of the scorched earth. The wheels spun with an inexorable bounce and clatter and the horses' hoofs made quiet thunder, while the great revolving copper blades began to hum. Kemheb was sitting at Thurms' feet, one arm wrapped about his left leg, holding Thurms' bow ready for him. The curving leather jackets protected their flanks but left a slot in the rear and one in the front through which Thurms could manage the team and shoot arrows.

Standing his full height on the rattling platform, his neck, head and helmet rising above the leather armor, Thurms watched the Khabiri hurrying toward them as though they were a united and mobile wall.

A fortress wall—bright and glinting their shields and spearpoints.

They began to run, spreading out, some in confusion as though not certain of the chariot's intended course. Thurms could hear their war cries now; their bodies were beginning to take on individual shape and dimension, their bearded faces assuming features; and five, six, a dozen arrows needled the heat-wavy air. He felt Kemheb's arm tighten on his leg.

Swiss-sss-sh—tunktunktunk! against the leather armor. Thurms crouched, pulling his head in like a turtle drawing into its shell, and suddenly veered the team to the right, cutting obliquely into the running, gesticulating Khabiri. A pandemonium of waving arms, flying legs, shaking spears, sun-glinting shields and screaming violence tore the air with insanity. The chariot bounced and lurched, bolted forward careening wildly, the copper blades going *knak-knak-knak!*

A spear whacked the metal helmet from his head; an arrow whickered in and glanced off his tabbed corselet; the right wheel met something with a slam, bouncing the chariot in a high sickening tilt, and for a moment Thurms thought they were going over.

They crashed down, rocking violently, skidded sideways to a near halt, and then they were rolling again, cutting a fresh path through the screaming Khabiri.

The chariot was clear for the moment: it had smashed through the first barrier . . . but scattered little groups of Khabiri were running before and around them. Thurms snatched for the bow, seeing three men forming a spear phalanx before the charging team. Quickly they grounded the butts of their spears, leaned their bodies back on the hafts, ready to transfix the team like a melon rolling onto a knifeblade.

Thurms had time to fire but one arrow before he had to swerve the team, clipping one of the remaining two spearmen with the off horse. Immediately he was confronted with another phalanx trap and swerved again, trying to throw them off in a flanking sweep. The snicker-snack of the spinning copper blades sparked a chill in his backbone as they lurched into the clear again and charged for the hills.

The towering battlements of the rocky hills seemed to roll

up and over them like a great gray wave. The pass was choked with yelling Khabiri and the arrow flights darkened the air. Everywhere Thurms looked stood a spear phalanx.

His only strategy was to charge straight at the spears, as though meaning to take them head-on, and then at the last split second to swerve right or left, striking them aside with the team's padded flanks and with the whirring copper blades.

They hit the bristling, billowing wall—swerving, skidding, the whicker-whack of the blades vibrating the axle until he was certain it would throw off the platform, leaving them smashed and helpless in the savage mob.

Something burning like fire knifed along his cheek, tore his ear and was gone. A javelin went *whamp!* coming half through the leather armor, and he flinched back as a spear jutted before his face, and saw it vanish as the heavy jackets ripped it aside and the chariot lurched on. It was time, he decided desperately, to reach into the grab bag of gods.

Ten times ten gold chains to Ammon if the horses may only stand, he vowed, and added, *And an equal amount to Aton . . .* merely to be on the safe side.

Suddenly he was aware of a rhythmic hum in the copper blades and—the rocky slopes of the pass flashing, leaping, falling on either side—he realized they had broken through.

A following hail of arrows whickered down from the hills, and Thurms—jubilant, exhilarated with action, nerves and triumph—raised his head and saw the flicker of someone he thought he recognized on the left bank.

The last he saw of Azmachis was the tragicomic scene of the fat one down on his knees throwing handfuls of dirt in his hair. The chariot clattered gaudily through the pass, drawing the enraged Khabiri cries down to a thin vanishing point.

3

A LINE ON TENAKERTOM

They didn't stop until they reached Azira's Well. There Thurms checked the horses for wounds—finding many but none overly serious—doctored them to the best of his ability, watered them, and then removed the copper blades from the wheels. He cleaned them in the sand and buried them by the well to be retrieved by a later patrol. Then he stripped the leather jackets from the chariot.

Kemheb sat in the palm shade eating dates, watching Thurms speculatively.

"We'll let the team have a good rest, then we'll get on to the garrison at Daphnae," Thurms said, coming over to sit beside his friend in the cool sand. A sharp look passed over Kemheb's thin face, and he merely nodded. Thurms studied him puzzledly.

"Kemheb—who are you, really?"

"Really?" The youth gave a small mysterious smile. "I'm an adventurer, Thurms. I follow the rumored but intangible. I seek the far-off and forgotten."

"Adventure?" Thurms echoed. "What would you call that

which we just experienced?" Kemheb shook his head disparagingly.

"That was war, and war is not a true adventure. It is a substitute. There is no adventure to a bloody head-on encounter between two armies; that's simply folly. No, adventure is man pitting himself against the magnitude and mysteries of nature, seeking the unknown, following the world's lost paths to their hidden conclusions." His bright green eyes flashed at Thurms.

"Have you ever heard of Tenakertom?" His voice was a hushed voice.

There was the familiar word again. Thurms wrinkled his brow.

"Y-e-s, I think so. Somewhere, sometime . . ."

Kemheb grinned. "You've spent too much time in garrisons, Thurms, besieging your brain with military theories, and not enough time in daydreaming. Azmachis—believe it or not—is a daydreamer, though of a different brand than myself. His dreams are of greed. But *he* has heard of Tenakertom, and that is why I was so important to him."

"Well, what is this accursed Tenakertom?"

"A lost city, Thurms. Reputedly, a lost treasure city."

Thurms raised a hand to his mouth to scoff. "Childishness," he stated. "Intangible smoke dreams for those who are too lazy to work or fight for their bread."

"Ah, but where there is smoke there is fire, or the dying embers of a fire," Kemheb reminded him. "At least, so thought one of my eccentric ancestors. At the close of the 17th Dynasty he and his mute Nubian slave set out to find the lost city. My adventurous ancestor was never seen again, but four years later his slave returned alone to Thebes. He had with him a papyrus scroll upon which his master had inscribed certain directions for finding Tenakertom, but they were vague and dealt with the names of places no one had ever heard of. The slave himself was of no help, of course, for he couldn't speak and he had never learned how to write. No one ever knew of the fate that had befallen his master.

"And it would seem that everyone in my family since then was a skeptic—just like you. None of them had enough interest in the mysterious and the marvelous to attempt to follow the directions in the old scroll—until I rediscovered it among some old family records a month ago. Immediately I knew what I must do and I ran off from home to do it. But I made a drastic mistake in Tanis: I trusted a stranger—Azmachis. He was posing as a horse and donkey trader and I made arrangements with him for a team of pack animals to transport me into Sinai.

"Seeing that I knew nothing at all about Sinai, and because Azmachis professed a great knowledge of the land, I showed him a portion of the scroll and asked for his help and advice. That was my mistake. That wily rogue must have guessed immediately that I had somehow come upon a line to Tenakertom. When I realized from his agitated and crafty manner that I had stepped into deep water, I pretended that I had changed my mind, that I was no longer interested in the journey. As soon as I was out of his sight I tore the scroll to bits and scattered them. But that night his minions caught me in a lonely alley and I was spirited away to the Wilderness of Shur."

The tale was interesting enough but Thurms still didn't see that it proved anything. "Kemheb, do you believe that this Tenakertom really exists?"

"Exists? Of course it exists. Everything you've ever dreamed of exists." Then, with a smile, Kemheb added, "When you're my age you'll understand that." He waved a hand toward the direction of the great desert of Sinai.

"Listen, Thurms, somewhere out there, lost among the

trackless dunes, there is an old old well—Seken's Well—and from its rim may be seen Anar's Arch. And that is the key."

"The key to what, for Set's sake?"

"To Tenakertom, to the statue of Tanit, the goddess who ruled the Delta in ancient times."

He didn't know why, but for a disturbing moment Thurms was stirred by Kemheb's infectious enthusiasm. His mind activated the imagery of a forbidden gorge in a mysterious mountain range, sheltering a dead city that was inhabited by the wraiths of old warriors, and he saw a huge weathered statue standing forlornly in the central wind-swept square, surrounded by deep vast timeless silence.

Kemheb watched him shrewdly. "Can you see it, Thurms? Can you see that long-lost caravan of treasure plodding on and on toward the Gebel Yelleq Range?"

Caravan . . . a magical word, a word that paints vivid mental pictures of camels with tassels and tinkling bells, and gaunt hawk-nosed men with faces veiled from the blowing sand, and tall wobbling jars of rare oils and perfumes and carefully wrapped objects of gold and swaying packs of precious gems; a motley procession of standard-bearers, fan-bearers, soldiers, musicians and priests . . . Caravan, a word from the dreams of youth.

Thurms came down to earth and to Azira's desert well with a start. He glanced sheepishly at the watchful Kemheb. He knew what his trouble had been a moment ago: crafty Kemheb had let loose a gold bug and it had started to nibble at the impulsive youth which Thurms kept hidden inside his man-soldier's body. In fact, it had nearly given him a good hard bite.

He grinned crookedly at Kemheb and shook his head. "You nearly had me started there; but then I'm not myself today. I'm very weary . . . hardly any sleep last night . . ." He yawned, stretching back in the soft blue-shadowed sand.

"Now be serious, Kemheb. Who are you really? The commander at Daphnae is a taciturn soldier who never indulges in fanciful or illusory thinking. And now that you and I have kicked up a little desert war, he'll want to know why—why Azmachis and his tribesmen think you are so important."

Kemheb was staring out at the heat-shimmering desert. He seemed to have lost all interest in the conversation. His voice was toneless.

"Then suppose we leave it up to the commander at Daphnae. I have nothing more to say about myself."

Thurms shrugged. He felt too beat to argue about it. He closed his heavy-lidded eyes, to rest for just a moment.

Oddly enough he saw it again—the tag end of that tireless caravan plodding on, on, before the dawn of history, moving away from him across the shifting sands, passing beyond the smooth-rolling horizon of dunes. And, for just a moment, he thought one of those long-lost rearguard soldiers turned and looked back at him from the crown of the furthestmost sand hill and raised a javelin to him as though in salute—or perhaps beckoning. *Come on. Come on. Follow after . . .*

It was early noon when Thurms awoke with a start, his soldier's instinct instantly alert and wary.

He was alone at Azira's Well. Quite alone. Kemheb was gone.

So was the team and the chariot. Kemheb had left him a waterskin by the well. He had also left a message in a smoothed-out place in the sand. It was written from right to left in a fine hieratic hand.

> Thurms, forgive me. I had to go on. Should you ever understand the difference between adventure and war, then remember the Key.

An arrow had been drawn in the sand. Its barbed head pointed southeast. Thurms straightened up to follow it with his eye. He stood there for a long time, immobilely, staring straight out into the empty heart of the desert of Sinai.

4

AKHETATON

It was good to be on the Nile again, to be back in Egypt proper. It would be even better if the ship he was on were bearing him upriver to Thebes, the city of his birth, but it wasn't. It was only taking him as far as Akhetaton—Horizon-of-Aton—a wonderful new city which Pharaoh had had built for himself and his god.

Thurms was on a mission for Bek—a rather dubious one, he feared, from his standpoint.

He had not had to walk the long scorching distance back to Daphnae from Azira's Well. Bek, annoyed by Thurms' and Hritut's failure to return from patrol, had sent out a chariot to investigate. Thurms had been escorted hurriedly to headquarters and into Bek's irate presence.

"Where is your good friend Hritut?" Bek had snapped.

Thurms had explained.

"Indeed. And where is this slave whom you took prisoner?"

Thurms had explained.

"Ah? And where is the tablet which the Syrian merchant gave you?"

Thurms had explained that the tablet had gone the way of the chariot, the team, Hritut and Kemheb. Bek had blown out his breath and pulled at his craggy nose which had once been broken in some warlike encounter.

"So," he said, or growled. "It wasn't enough that Egypt has a war breaking out with the Khabiri in Syria. *You* had to start one in Sinai—right at our doorstep—for a mere worthless slave boy. Thurms, are you certain that you're a general's son and not an *idiot's* son?"

"Yes sir—I mean, I'm certain I'm not an idiot's son."

"Then what made you adopt this idiotic course of action?"

"Well, there were certain indications that Kemheb was telling the truth and that Azmachis was lying."

"What indications?"

"Well, they're rather vague, I'll admit. Azmachis' manner mostly, and one other thing: Kemheb claimed that Azmachis knew that he, Kemheb, was in possession of a valuable secret."

"What secret?"

"The secret about a mythical place called Tenakertom."

Something happened in Bek's hard-set, desert-squinted eyes. Thurms thought he detected a spark of interest. Yet Bek's naturally harsh voice, when he asked his next question, was casual enough.

"What did the boy think he knew about this place called Tenakertom?"

Thurms was mildly surprised that Bek was willing to wander away from the subject of the Khabiri attack to explore the illusory futilities of an old myth.

"Only something vague about a place called Seken's Well and something about an archway which could be seen from the well."

Bek said *hmm* and looked thoughtful. Then he had

reached for a roll of burnished papyrus and a reed pen. Dipping the pen into an alabaster palette, which contained black and red pigments, he began to write in a broad soldierly hand—which probably left much to be desired from a reader's viewpoint. Using a small inscribed cylinder to seal the document in Pharaoh's name, he handed the roll to Thurms.

"I'm sending you to Akhetaton, Thurms. Your father the General is there with Pharaoh. Give this report to your father. If it has the effect I hope it will he will attempt to reason with that weak-willed fool we have for a king, and then perhaps he will be condescending enough to send us an army to fight these Maut-cursed Khabiri, before they take Syria, Sinai, and the Delta too. That is all."

Thurms had paused at the doorway. "I—uh wonder, sir, if this report makes any mention of my part in the Azmachis incident?"

Bek pulled at the nose on his adamantine face which nothing could ever really damage again, and said coldly and with finality:

"That is all." And Thurms had departed for the Nile none the wiser for his inopportune question.

He enjoyed his voyage up the Nile. The ship was of the best design, the steering oar being equipped with a rudder post and tiller (a 6th Dynasty invention), and the comfortable leather-covered cabin in the stern was entirely at his disposal, seeing that he was a military envoy to Pharaoh. The two-legged mast with its huge one-piece sail had been unstepped and the Nubian crew was bending lustily to the oars.

They stroked by the papyrus pools of the Delta where families were duck hunting from skiffs of bundled papyrus reeds with boomerangs, holding small captured herons in their left hands as decoy birds; and where fowlers worked in teams in the marshes netting wild geese, pintail ducks, and widgeons. The fowlers were using the most common device for catching these birds alive—the large clapnet.

The fowlers would bait a small pool and spread flat a two-halved net, the inner edges hinged on staked cords and the outer edges secured to anchored draw ropes. When the wildfowl landed in the pool a lookout man would give the signal and the fowlers manning the draw rope would spring the trap, swinging the wings of the net up, over, and down on the fluttering birds.

The ship made its way by the shores of El Giza where, the receding waters of the yearly Nile flood having left the fields damp, the farmers were already planting their winter crop of barley and wheat. Sowers walked slowly across the muddy fields shedding seeds from their bags and hands as they went, followed by teams of long-horned African cows drawing plows to turn the seed under.

But they were only farmers and Thurms had the soldier's hearty contempt for all such dull clodhopping civilians. What interested him more was the spectacle that rose on the desert plateau beyond the toiling farmers and their beasts— the huge, triangular, throat-clutching pyramids of Cheops, Khaefre and Menkaure. The three kings of the 4th Dynasty, father, son, and grandson.

For some reason (perhaps because these monumental tombs were known to house unapproachable and utterly unobtainable treasures) Thurms' mind side-slipped to a vision of Kemheb—that thin, boyish, gallant enigma who was playing a very dangerous game against man and the forces of nature. And he asked himself the question which he had pondered over and which had plagued him for three days and nights now.

Did Tenakertom really exist?

At Abusir he saw the great solar obelisk and sun temple

built by Pharaoh Newosere in the 5th Dynasty (2500 B.C.). It was far far off across the bulrushes and marshy pools, remote and separate, seemingly, from mankind and his accumulative and—in the scheme of things—minor problems. It shone like rose gold in the late sun.

At Memphis the ship glided by a mastaba field—a City of the Dead. This form of tomb monument was for distant members of the royal family, nobles and officials in high standing. Laid out like streets in a town the tombs were rectangular, flat-topped affairs made of stone. Thurms' father said that they were the direct evolvement from the crude mounds of sand and earth heaped over the prehistoric graves.

And there were crocodiles, everywhere: the independent and exceedingly voracious 'disposal units' of the Nile. Thurms liked to watch their peculiarly corroded and pitted heads emerge from the green depths of the river and open their huge traplike jaws, showing their multitude of fearsome dentures, to hiss wetly and hungrily and challengingly after the ship.

It was said that, like the tiger, the crocodile acquired a taste for human beings, and Thurms could readily believe it because the reptilian monsters were forever skirting along the shores of the Nile looking for washerwomen, swimming children, and careless bathers.

When a crocodile caught an unwary victim (man or beast) he began a tugging, yanking, backward motion, like a playful dog taking you on in a game of tug-of-war with a piece of cloth or bit of cord. If he could get his victim into the deep water he would take it down to a submerged root along the riverbank and wedge it there and hold it there, until it drowned, and leave it there, snagged in the root, for a few days until it was ripe and tasty, and then . . .

That was the Nile—wild, primitive, savage, on one side

of the coin; cultivated, industrious, civilized on the other. It all depended on which way the coin fell; and to Thurms it always stood on edge, half and half. But then, all the world was like that . . . and perhaps it would always remain so. Just like that.

Akhetaton was a dream city—literally. It had nothing of the aspect of reality about its flowering, fragile splendor. Palm trees nodded along its emaculate streets, vivid blossoms bloomed like little explosions in its multitude of gardens, and one had to be careful where one stepped or one would unwittingly step into a fish pool cleverly concealed under a bed of floating lotus flowers; indeed, there seemed to be more fish pools than streets.

The houses themselves seemed brittle and impermanent, being made of wood and open to the Nile zephyrs in the manner of pavilions. Pharaoh's palace was like a light and airy summer residence. Its long front verandah with its brightly painted lotus-bud columns overlooked a large lotus pool bordered with mandrake, oleander, jasmine and dwarf chrysanthemums. Ranged around the walls were rows of fig trees and the tall date and dom palms.

A myriad of gaily playing children were in the garden, boys and girls: many of them not much younger than Thurms. They paused in their games to stare at him with unabashed curiosity and speculation, and he felt rough and embarrassed in their innocent unworldly presence. Then he spotted someone he knew.

It was Tutankhamon, Pharaoh's youngest son-in-law, a strange moody bemused youth of sixteen. He and Thurms had been playfellows long ago in Thebes.

Tutankhamon was off in one corner of the garden by himself sitting in the bindweed and cornflowers, playing with model pyramids and mastabas and little doll mummies in sarcophaguses. Overall, his play area gave off a rather tombish effect. He was conducting a mock funeral ceremony.

"Tut," Thurms greeted his old friend. "How do I find you?"

Tutankhamon looked up as though he were not quite certain that he and Thurms were of this world. He spoke in a grave voice.

"Thurms? I remember you. You went off to war."

"Well, not really," Thurms said candidly. "Only to the desert—"

"Have you seen much killing in the desert, Thurms? Many dead men? How do they process the bodies in the desert?" Tutankhamon had suddenly become quite animated. Thurms looked down at him blankly.

"I—I wouldn't know, Tut. I've only been in one battle."

Tutankhamon's attention had wandered. He picked up one of the toy mummies. "I'm burying this official today," he murmured. "He was but a tax-gatherer and so I can only give him a common mastaba. His tomb will be nothing compared to the one I am planning for myself."

"Yourself?" Thurms felt a tingling in the nape of his neck.

"Yes. It will be the most costly tomb ever constructed. But not a pyramid. I won't have the grave robbers disturbing me in my eternal rest. I plan on hiding my tomb in the Valley of the Kings. It will be so well concealed that it will take mankind thousands of years to discover me. And when they finally do they will find that I and my treasures are as intact and preserved as the day we were sealed up. And then my name shall become immortal!"

King Tut, Thurms reflected. He tried to picture a far-removed generation digging deep into the Egyptian earth to find this strangely morbid youth.

"Pharaoh, my father-in-law, is not a well man." Tutankhamon seemed to be conversing with himself. "He has not long to live. Sekenre, his oldest son-in-law, is stupid beyond all reason or belief. The wise high priests will see to it that he does not remain Pharaoh for long. Then I shall become Pharaoh of Egypt! And I shall send forth all my tax-gatherers to amass for me a great fortune so that I might begin at once to build my tomb of immortality!"

Thurms, looking emptily at Tutankhamon—who had once laughed happily and played the game 'going round four times' with him—felt a sense of loss. Once they had been children together. Now Thurms was seventeen and a soldier and Egypt counted upon him as a man. And Tutankhamon? He was still a child—a lonely little boy with a macabre obsession for death.

"Farewell, Tut," Thurms said quietly. "Perhaps I will see you again." But the morbid youth had already forgotten about Thurms. He was busy lowering the 'tax-gatherer' into his model tomb.

The General received his son in his private room in the royal palace. He was a stocky, iron-eyed, imposing figure of a man: every inch a soldier. He wore the usual fillet of colored cloth on his head with the ends flowing over his burly shoulders. It was held in place with a serpentlike coil of gold around his forehead. A silver-handled dagger was lashed to his left upper arm and it was of the Hyksos design, as was the bronze war axe which he kept tucked in his belt. He looked at his son as a general should look at a son who is also a soldier.

"Well, Thurms, I must confess that I am surprised to see you here."

Thurms was never quite certain whether he should address his father as Father or as General. He decided upon an intermediary 'sir.'

"I am here under Commander Bek's orders, sir." He drew the roll of papyrus from his belt and handed it to the General.

The stern warrior perused the document carefully, his eyes sharpening, widening, sharpening again. Once he looked up with a mildly incredulous expression.

"Bek says that you and a slave boy were attacked by two or three hundred Khabiri and fought your way through them. Is this true?"

Thurms admitted that it was true, and the General's hard eyes took on a glow of warmth. "But how—with only an open chariot?"

Thurms explained the details, and this time the General's craggy face actually beamed. "Truly? You armored your chariot with horse pads? That's rather ingenious, Thurms. In fact, you might just have innovated something which could be used as a future military weapon."

Thurms was beginning to feel very pleased with himself —until the General read on. "What's this? What's this?" The General looked up again, his face not quite as bright as before.

"Your charioteer deserted while you were on guard?"

Thurms cleared his throat. "I—uh dozed off for a moment."

"While *on guard?*" the General insisted.

Thurms glanced up at the vividly painted ceiling, and nodded.

The General couldn't believe what he next discovered in the report.

"Thurms! It says here you later lost your chariot, your team, *and* your prisoner. It says you were *sleeping* again and you let the slave boy run off with everything except the uniform you were wearing!"

Thurms took in his breath. "Well, sir, I hadn't had much sleep for—"

"Thurms! I sent you to the desert to learn how to become a soldier! *Not* to discover sleeping sickness!"

All in all it was a most painful interview, and Thurms was greatly relieved when it finally terminated with the General telling him sharply to remain where he was.

"I must report to Pharaoh. It is possible that he will wish to see you. If he does—make some attempt to stay *awake* in his presence!"

Miserably, Thurms promised to do his best.

An hour later he was ushered into Pharaoh's audience hall by his glowering father. Then his father departed, and Thurms found himself alone with Akhnaton and his pet lion. Pharaoh was sitting on a throne dais which was built in the form of a ramp. The lion was sprawled at his feet, licking his chops, eying Thurms sleepily.

Thurms threw himself on the floor before Pharaoh according to custom, at the same time wishing that the custom could be changed—or at least that the floors could be kept cleaner.

"Rise," Akhnaton said over him. "Approach."

The truth was, Thurms didn't really want to approach. He already felt too close to the dais for comfort. That lion, he thought, had a sort of hungry look in its baleful eye.

Akhnaton was not an old man, he merely looked that way; a thin, weak, sickly-constructed man with strangely harassed eyes. He said:

"Your father tells me you are from the Delta and the desert."

"Yes, Lord," Thurms admitted, idly wondering if he would have time to shin up one of the nearby colored lotus columns, should the royal pet suddenly decide to make an untoward move.

"Tell me, Thurms," Akhnaton said with sudden eagerness, "what do the Delta people think of my new god Aton? Is he well received in the Lower Kingdom?"

"Well—" Thurms said cautiously, "I spend most of my time on patrol in the desert. I hardly have time to talk with the Delta—"

"And what do the men of the desert think of Aton?"

"The Khabiri?" Thurms tried to picture the savagely visaged tribesmen thinking about Aton. But it didn't work. The picture wouldn't come into focus. "Well—"

"The trouble with Egypt is that we are plagued with too many gods." Akhnaton, like his son-in-law Tut, gave the impression that he frequently talked to himself, even when other people were standing nearby. He began checking the gods off on his fingers.

"Osiris, Isis, Horus, Hathor, Nephthys, Ra, Ptah, Maut, Set, Anubis—" running out of fingers, he switched back to his left hand and started with his forefinger again, "—Thoth and Ammon. This is confusing and unnecessary. It has been my intent to do away with this hodge-podge of false gods, to bring my people to realize that there is only one god. Aton." He gave Thurms a penetrating look.

"You understand what I am saying? There is only *one* god. He created *every*thing: you, me, this lion, the world and everything in it, down to the smallest grain of sand in the desert. He is totally without form and he is everywhere at once. He is with those children playing in the gardens. He is with you when you are on your lonely patrol in Sinai. He is here. In this room. Now. With us."

Akhnaton hesitated, looked up and around with a strange bright light in his sunken eyes. So did Thurms. And—oddly —so did the lion.

"If he has an image," Akhnaton continued in a hushed voice, "it is a circle with hands, many hands—like the sun with its rays of light, blessing everything he touches. And most important—to Aton, all men are equal: slave and Pharaoh alike."

It was a strange conception; but, oddly enough, it seemed almost reasonable to Thurms. One god. Formless. Who had created everything, and who saw no difference between slave and noble. It was a rather comfortable idea.

Thurms came back to himself and realized that Pharaoh was regarding Bek's document with a moody expression.

"Now this Commander Bek, *and* your father, are imploring me to send an army into Sinai and Syria, to make war on those simple desert folk. Can they not realize that Aton does not believe in war?"

"Forgive me, Lord, but the Khabiri are not simple desert folk. They are warlike savages who mean to lay Syria to utter waste."

"But I believe in peace," Akhnaton insisted. "War is abominable!"

"Perhaps so," Thurms conceded. "But war is sometimes necessary."

Akhnaton fluttered the papyrus report impatiently. "That is quibbling. I detest quibbling. A thing is either right or it isn't! I must dwell upon it. I must think . . ." His voice went off quietly and became lost in the wan silence of the room.

"Sir," Thurms ventured, "if the Khabiri are not stopped—"

But Pharaoh was no longer listening, no longer aware of Thurms' presence or existence. He appeared to be deeply sunken in some personal reverie. The lion regarded Thurms steadily.

Thurms didn't know what to do with himself. So he decided to withdraw quietly. He turned and walked away. When he looked back he saw that the lonely brooding Pharaoh and his lion were sitting exactly as he had left them, like a pair of royal statues.

That evening the General entered Thurms' room with the look of a thundercloud. "Prepare for another journey," he said crisply.

"To where, sir?"

"Back to Daphnae. Pharaoh has decided to send General Horemheb to Sinai to do something about the Khabiri. Horemheb has been acting as Pharaoh's household bodyguard and he is embarking immediately. You, however, will leave tonight with a report for Bek, so that he will know what preparations to make to receive Horemheb."

"Then it's to be war!" Thurms cried.

The General's face went sour. "War? Well, perhaps Pharaoh would so term it, but I'd give it another name—slaughter. Egyptian slaughter."

Thurms said that he didn't understand. His father grunted.

"How many Khabiri would you say there are in Syria and Sinai?"

Thurms threw his hands in the air. "The patrol veterans say that the Khabiri are as many as the sands of the desert."

The General nodded glumly.

"And against this countless horde Horemheb will be allowed to take one squadron of chariots and two thousand archers and spearmen. And that is his 'army.' "

5

A CROC FOR KIPA

THURMS SPENT most of his time restlessly pacing the deck of the ship that bore him down the Nile. He was appalled by Pharaoh's mad decision to attempt to fight a bloodless war with the Khabiri. Pharaoh—caught between his obsession for peace and the need to save Syria and Sinai from the barbarians—had come up with a compromise that was next to worthless.

Thurms couldn't see how Horemheb could possibly accomplish more than a routine police action in Sinai with only sixty chariots and two thousand foot soldiers. At best Bek might be able to scrape together half a squadron of chariots; and still it would be like trying to sweep the ocean from the shore with a dog-eared rush broom.

No wind prevailing, the ship was under oars and skirting the western shore of the Nile. Idly Thurms leaned on the cedarwood rail and contemplated the sliding landscape and its river inhabitants. On nearly every stretch of beach that was free of bulrushes washerwomen squatted and scrubbed and gossiped to their hearts' content, while their offspring bathed or gamboled gaily in the shallows around them.

Near one such active group Thurms noticed a ball-shaped man in the head-to-foot woolen gown of a Syrian. He was standing in the knee-high shallows bathing his feet, his back foolishly to the river. He had tucked his skirts up carefully in front but—unknown to him—they had slipped down in back and were trailing in the water.

Suddenly Thurms snapped to rapt attention. The familiar corrugated snout of a crocodile was gently rising to the surface directly behind the unsuspecting footbather.

"Hi! *You!* Beware!" Thurms shouted, and immediately all the people along the shore, as well as the Nubian oarsmen on board the ship, looked up. So did the fool standing in the water with his back to the Nile—*up* but not down, where the swift-gliding danger was.

"You called?" he inquired with an innocent smile.

Thurms, his eyes starting from his head, pointed wildly. "There! There! *Right behind you, man!*"

The Syrian-garbed man, who was as rotund as a tub of butter, glanced down and saw the fifteen-foot reptilian horror knifing for his legs, its upper jaw already unhinging and rising to present its toothy display, and he let out a cry that could well have disturbed Cheops in his pyramid. He took off for the mudbank, highstepping through the shallows like a man running barefoot through eggs.

But not quick enough.

The tail of his flowing robes was dragging in the water behind him, and the crocodile gave a half-hitch with its great laterally-compressed tail and shot forward and brought its traplike jaws together with a slam on the tailpiece of the soggy garments, and the fat man was stopped so short and sudden in his frantic flight that he almost went ankles over appetite backwards.

Immediately the croc went into its tugging yanking backing motion, foot by foot dragging the helpless yelling man into the deeper water. There was one thing in the victim's favor, however—the bole of an ancient broken palm jutting from the shallows like a black snaggle tooth. The fat man grabbed it, wrapping both arms tightly around the stub of trunk. The croc increased the back-thrust of its yanking.

The washerwomen and the children on the shore simply didn't know what to do except help the unhappy man scream. The glassy Nile air became a pandemonium of noise. And all the Nubian sailors did was stand along the rail shouting unhearable advice to the luckless victim, none of it very valid for a man in his dire situation.

Thurms made a grimace with his mouth, snatched out his sword, and took a hand-on-the-rail swinging jump over the side. He came down in four feet of water, his face crashing under, then bobbed up again as he found firm footing.

The tip of the slowly lashing tail of the croc was two yards in front of him. He started to wade forward, edging off to the left. The croc back-rolled its eye and spotted him coming. Instantly it scurried around, sighting on Thurms, swung up its tail and brought it down against the water like the fall of an obelisk, and again and again, striking here, there, and in between.

It was the most monstrous thing Thurms had ever seen in a wild state. Not that fifteen feet was as long as crocs came—but it was four feet wide and half that thick. It was a grandfather, greenish-yellow with age and with a mosslike fungus on its back. Wise with the wisdom of Nile ages, it watched Thurms with blinkless concentration.

If Thurms moved to the left the croc would pivot its body in the same direction and take another warning strike at him with its tail. The same thing happened if Thurms shifted to the right. He couldn't get by the treacherous scut-plated thing.

"*Do something! Do something!*" the fat man wailed. "Do you expect me to hug this accursed palm forever?" Then Thurms lost his temper.

"I expect you to keep your windy mouth closed, or I'll go back to the ship and let you play with the crocodile by yourself!"

"Don't do it! Don't do it! Kind good helpful brave sir! By all the potters' wheels—large and small—not another word shall pass my lips, should my life depend upon it!"

"It might at that!" Thurms took a deep breath and submerged himself. The water in the shallows was fairly translucent and, blurredly, he could make out the undulating tail and hindquarters of the great saurian directly in front of him.

He raised his legs and tipped his body downward, touching the oozy bottom with his left hand. His fingers found a sturdy root and he grabbed, held himself there.

The croc was apprehensive. It could no longer see its enemy. It swung the heavy tail laterally, cutting a wide foamy arc underwater, and Thurms saw the sweep coming and pulled his body down short with his left hand. He felt the compressible displacement of the swinging tail over his head and shoulders. Then he kicked forward for all he was worth, aiming for the croc's left hind leg before the tail could come crushing back.

Slipping, sliding, spewing water and gasping for air, he came up alongside the shifting tail-kicking brute and started to scramble onto the mossy scutellated back, still clutching the sword in his hand.

It was time for the croc to make a decisive move. By some trend of instinctual reasoning it must have known that the man on its back was coming for one of its eyes with the bright sharp thing. It opened its jaws, released the fat man's mangled garments and began a turning backing side-diving motion all practically in one movement.

Thurms, wobbling, clutching at nothing for support, rose on the rapidly shifting living platform and took a leap toward the shallows and the shore. The croc submerged with a rush, leaving a yellow welter of foam behind, all the sailors and washerwomen and children cheering excitedly.

Thurms, wading ashore, looked around and saw that the fat man was still clutching the palm trunk for dear life, his eyes closed and his mouth open, screaming bloody murder. Thurms went back and rapped him on his bald head.

"Stop that. There's no reason for all that unseemly noise."

The fat man's eyes popped open and glared at Thurms. *"Unseemly!* Well how would you like to have a crocodile hanging to your . . . oh. *OH!* It's you! Is the monster gone? Did we fight him off?"

"Yes," Thurms said dryly, "we fought him off. You may let go of the palm trunk now."

The fat man (rather pompously, Thurms thought) strutted from the water, rearranging his tattered, dripping, and already filthy garments, tagging after Thurms, saying that his name was Kipa, that he was a Syrian returning to his homeland on foot, and that he would be Thurms' slave for life.

Thurms regarded the talkative man shrewdly. Kipa didn't look, sound, or act like a Syrian. There was a sly, roguish quality to his moony face, mostly in his small bright porcine eyes. Thurms had an idea that Kipa (if that were truly his name) was either a runaway slave or an escaped convict from one of Pharaoh's mines in the south.

"Thank you. But I don't want or need a slave."

"You don't want or need a slave!" Kipa couldn't believe what he'd heard. "Why, everyone wants a slave! Even the slaves do! It's the Egyptian way of life!"

Thurms wished that Kipa wouldn't talk so boisterously. Everyone was gathering to listen. "Perhaps so, but it isn't my way. Besides, I can't afford to feed or clothe a slave."

"Can't afford to feed or clothe a slave! Of course you can! An important soldier like you!"

Thurms took him by the arm, led him away from the crowd.

"Must you shout the palms down? I can hear you very well from here. I'm not standing in Giza. And I tell you *I don't want a slave.*"

But it developed that Kipa had a theory about the crocodile incident. He, Thurms, had saved his, Kipa's, life . . . therefore he, Thurms, had to care and provide for him, Kipa, for the rest of his, Kipa or Thurms', natural life. It was all very simple and natural and proper and, as far as Kipa was concerned, it was settled. However, when Thurms persisted to decline this generous arrangement, Kipa went wild with despair.

Up and down the shore he ran, grabbing this grinning individual to shout, "He saves me from the crocodile's mouth only to throw me to starvation's maw!" Grabbing the next bewildered bystander to wail, "By Anubis and all his mangy watchdogs of the tombs, who has ever beheld such a heartless youth as this cruel soldier!" And he kept it up until finally Thurms (his face burning red) caught him and shook him and ordered him to stop making such a spectacle of himself.

Instantly Kipa was all fawning obedience. "Yes, good sweet master! Readily, master of masters! Shall we repair to the ship now and continue on our way to wherever it is we are going?"

"Perhaps this will come as a blow to you," Thurms said acidly. "But I believe that the bargemaster will require money for your passage, and my purse is nearly empty as it is . . ." He started feeling about his waist. His purse was missing.

Kipa smirked and winked and placed one dirty finger next to his nose slyly, and took a thin wet purse from somewhere within his capacious robes. Thurms' purse.

"I have already relieved you of the burden of carrying it about," he explained. "As your servant, you must now leave all matters of finance in my capable hands—especially matters that concern monetary haggling. Now, let us on to the ship and I shall have a quiet word or two with the greedy captain!"

There were other passengers aboard the ship and now that Kipa had gone off with the bargemaster to the stern to discuss matters of finance (a discussion which quickly evolved into a gambling game known as Throwing the Sticks), one of them approached Thurms.

He was a small dark obsequious man with troublesome eyes—troublesome in that they couldn't seem to retain their focus on any given object for more than a second or two but were forever batting about like two swallows trapped in a stable. He sidled up to Thurms with a tentative smile.

"Kind soldier, I desire a measure of your protection," he said in a whisper that was nearly lost in the immensity of the river.

Thurms nodded dutifully. "You're welcome to it."

"A thousand thanks! It is a small favor, really. I fear thieves."

"Here? On this small ship?"

"The Nubian sailors," the man hastened to explain. "Rascals, all of them! I know, for I have made many voyages upon the Nile. All that I require of you is that you will retain a personal object for me for the night." So saying, he slid a curious- and costly-looking armlet down his arm and slipped it off his hand.

"It has great sentiment value for me. My mother gave it to me. It has been handed down from parent to child in my family for many generations. It belonged to my dear dear great-great-grandmother who was a handmaiden of Queen Hatshepsut."

"But surely no one could remove it from your arm without your being aware of it," Thurms reasoned. "Even if you were asleep."

The little man's nervous eyes lighted here, there, everywhere.

"You don't know how these Nubian villains work, Lord. In the night when you are asleep on the deck one of them sits himself upon your head so that you may not cry out, while another plants a dagger deep into your heart. Then they rob you and slip your corpse over the side and let the crocodiles dispose of it. But you, O soldier, have nothing to fear, for you sleep in the great cabin and may bar the door. And, too, you have your trusted servant to guard you and your valuables."

Thurms was inclined to smile wryly at the extravagant use of the word 'trusted' in regard to that king of rascals Kipa. Still and all, he reflected, he didn't see how Kipa—in his zeal to relieve Thurms of all troublesome and valuable burdens—could remove the armlet in Thurms' sleep without removing his arm first.

"Very well. But only for the night. Tomorrow morning you must claim it back."

"Four thousand thanks, mighty warrior of Kem!" the little man cried as he shoved the armlet into Thurms' hand and scuttled rapidly away to mingle with the other passengers forward.

Mighty warrior of Kem . . . the expression had the ring of familiarity. Who had given him that same salutation just recently? Frowning, he fell to studying the armlet. It was a thick gold coil with a jackal's head and a single red ruby eye. It was a snug fit on his right biceps and the tall jackal ears came to the point of his shoulder.

He found Kipa alone in the master cabin, reclining on the rush pillows which were intended for Thurms' bed. Instantly Kipa's avaricious eyes clamped onto the armlet.

"Master! Master! You have come into a fortune! Truly Thoth the god of wisdom knew what he was about when he sent you to me today!"

"Don't be silly. I'm merely keeping it for a passenger so that he won't have it stolen from him in the night."

"Excellent!" Kipa clapped his hands. "We shall sell it in the open market in Tanis the moment we land!"

"We shall do no such thing. It has been intrusted to my care, and I shall return it to its rightful owner in the morning."

Kipa covered his face with his hands, as if the sight of Thurms' naked folly was too much for him to bear. Thurms gave him a rap on the head.

"Stop that and tell me of your arrangements with the bargemaster. Has your passage been settled?"

Kipa removed his hands from his smirking face. "Oh yes."

"Well, was it costly? Have we any coins left in the purse?"

"Oh yes."

"Well, how many?" Thurms cried impatiently. "Enough to feed ourselves when we reach Tanis?"

"Enough I think." Kipa drew the purse—that Thurms used to call his own—from his cloak. Thurms was amazed to see that it had taken on a great deal of weight since he had last laid eyes on it.

"Did I not say you must leave all matters of finance in your servant's capable hands?" Kipa said in a sickeningly sweet voice. "I have many talents, Lord. I will prove useful to you in many ways. You have already observed the remarkable dexterity of my hands, eh?"

Thurms nodded. "I have observed that you are a pickpocket, yes."

Kipa placed his forearm across his eyes to ward off the insult.

"I also dabble in soothing," he announced. "I read the sands."

Read the sands . . . the phrase caught in Thurms' mind and revolved. He thought of Kemheb and his lonely desert quest. "Kipa," he said on impulse, "have you ever heard of Tenakertom?"

It was obvious from the effects that the word produced that Kipa had indeed heard of Tenakertom. He clawed at his bald head, at his ears. He positively drooled.

"Thurms, Thurms! You've been a patrol soldier in Sinai . . . is it possible that you've stumbled upon some clue in the sand regarding the lost city?"

Thurms couldn't see that there was anything to lose by telling the tale to Kipa, and so he did. Kipa listened with avid attention, mumbling the clues over and over to himself.

"Seken's Well—Anar's Arch—Gebel Yelleq Range—statue of Tanit—" He clapped his hands delightedly. "Ammon bless us! And Aton, too, of course. It is more than any adventurer has ever been given before!"

"But what does it all mean?"

"What does it all mean! Why that's simple enough. It means that we too must follow the Key to the riddle. First we reach the Range, then we find Seken's Well. The well shows us Anar's Arch, and the Arch takes us to Tanit's statue. Set's skillet! We'll be *rich rich rich!*"

"But how do we know there's a word of truth in the tale?"

"How do we know! How do we know! Simple-minded Thurms, ask yourself this question: would this Azmachis and his cutthroats start a desert war over a mere slave boy? Certainly not! Obviously Kemheb was telling the truth—he *had* been kidnaped. And I readily believe, master, that you arrived just in time to save your friend Kemheb from a nasty little taste of Khabiri torture."

Kipa lolled back on the pillows and pulled his ears in an ecstasy of excitement. "We shall find it, Thurms, son of good fortune! We shall sort the riddle out to our own satisfaction! Seken's Well . . . Anar's Arch . . ."

The gold bug was loose again. It was scrabbling about the cabin and it had already nearly devoured Kipa alive and now it was coming for Thurms. But he reminded himself that he was a soldier with a war on his hands and he kicked it off.

"Bar the door," he ordered bruskly. "I don't desire any visitors tonight. I must return this armlet to its owner in the morning."

But, when morning came, he found that he couldn't return it.

The owner was gone . . . no one seemed to know where or how.

6

GODS ARE DEVIOUS CREATURES

T ANIS WAS an old old city, and its incoming and outgoing roads were mapped by the ashy bones of beasts and men who had pursued them until they succumbed to thirst or hunger or heat or disease or just simple murder. It was ancient when Joseph came to Egypt and the Jews dated his arrival with the Hyksos kings. It was a yesterday city, for its prosperity and future were being destroyed by the silting up of the Tanitic mouth of the Nile. One day the filling up of the delta would result in its being left far inland. Then, slowly, it would be abandoned. And then, give or take a few centuries, it would become a lost city.

But not yet—not when Thurms and Kipa pushed their way along the crowded seething streets. The mud-walled hutments and minarets and mosques seemed to radiate heat like giant ovens, even though the narrow alleyways were covered overhead with fretworks of fronds to keep off the white hot African sun. It seemed a strange wild town, where life throbbed and pulsed in a way that was raw and curious and even a little wicked. It was home to Kipa. He expanded in its teaming sweaty sordidness. He strutted along with the anticipatory air of a man who expects to find his fortune waiting for him at the very next corner.

There were fourteen tall obelisks and many grand temples, the most enormous being the great temple to Set, the god of war. And so, in a soldierly way, it was home to Thurms too—but not a home he cared to dwell in overly long. The saffron and musk and burning charcoal and the savage perfume that the breeze fetched in from the sand hills to the southeast were too heady for his spartan nostrils.

Incense and ivory ornaments and cedarwood and ostrich feathers and fresh fish and newly baked bread and myrrh and brilliant-feathered talking birds, the gaudy woolen stuffs from Sidon and Byblos; agate-eyed robed men squatting in the gutters hawking their fly-haloed wares, their insistent voices hurling up like lariats of sound; camels plodding flat-footedly by, donkeys braying and twitching their ears, tidy little desert ponies prancing, chariots coming jobbity-jop, jobbity-jop heedlessly down the many-peopled streets . . .

And suddenly Thurms turned and looked behind him and saw a face in the crowd that brought him to a slamming halt.

Azmachis!

The Khabiri chieftain ducked his head and tried to plunge into the crowd to sink himself in the sea of humanity. But his first try was like trying to ram his hairy head through a mud-brick wall. Three riotous Egyptian soldiers repelled him, roughly shoving him back with good-natured insults and bad language.

"Stop that man!" Thurms yelled, but his voice was meaningless in the din of the commercial street. "Quick, Kipa! That's Azmachis!"

Without warning, a tall hawk-nosed man of great breadth stepped seemingly by accident into their path. Thurms collided with him and was jarred backward into the on-coming Kipa.

"Watch where you are going, desert rat," Hawknose snapped.

"My apologies," Thurms said hastily, and made a start around him. The man moved with alacrity, again blocking the way.

"Not so quickly, wolf's whelp," he said coldly. "You have given my person great insult."

Trying to see over Hawknose's shoulder and around him, Thurms spotted Azmachis' shaggy head plunging deeply into the crowd. In a moment he would lose him completely. Again he started around Hawknose, this time reaching out to straight-arm the man aside.

Hawknose stepped backwards hurriedly and darted a hand into his shoulder-to-ground robe. Kipa caught Thurms by the elbow and pulled him up short, as Hawknose drew a long black scorpion from his robe and held it before him as a weapon. The arachnid's caudal tail was curved up over its back, ready for angry business.

"I advise caution," Hawknose said in a low dangerous tone. "Attempt to touch me and you will catch my little friend in the face."

It seemed to Thurms to be a very effective method of holding an enemy in abeyance. But Azmachis was escaping. He sucked in his breath and reached for his sword.

Hawknose flipped the scorpion at Thurms' face—Thurms stumbling backward, throwing up a protective arm, ducking . . . but there was no need. Kipa, adroitly and calmly, snatched at the air and caught the tail-over-pincers spinning creature in his hand.

Thurms could only stand and gawk at Kipa, as the hawk-nosed man turned quickly and was swallowed by the crowd. Kipa joggled the scorpion in his hand and grinned at Thurms.

"I saw at first glance that the sting had been previously cut from the tail," he explained. "There's no more harm to this little devil than there is to a stylus with a blunt point."

Thurms threw his hands in the air in dismay. Azmachis had vanished down the gullet of Tanis. "Is it possible that he was following me?"

"Very possible. And very probable that he has his spies watching you all the time. After all, he has every reason to suspect that Kemheb has told you what he knows about Tenakertom."

Thurms grunted. "Yes, and that hawk-faced son of a Syrian . . . undoubtedly he too was one of Azmachis' lackeys."

"Undoubtedly, undoubtedly," Kipa mumbled, engrossed in the wiggling scorpion he held captive. "Thurms! Look at this rare treasure! This is no ordinary scorpion!"

Thurms thought it was—or nearly so. It was black and about five inches long and very bad-tempered. There was one outstanding feature, however: on the segmented post-abdomen was a curious and natural little diamond design of a rose-red hue.

"A god!" Kipa shouted. "The fool has thrown us a god! What luck! It will bring us an abundance of good fortune! Come, master, come! Let us find a secluded spot and put the god to a test."

Thurms, dubious and only half willing, followed Kipa to a sequestered and sand-floored sidecourt of an abandoned temple of Ra (a sun god of the early 18th Dynasty who had fallen into disfavor with the advent of Aton). He could understand Kipa's insistence that the scorpion was a god because such beliefs were very popular with the Egyptians; even General Horemheb kept a pet falcon which he claimed was his personal god.

Still—Thurms wished that if Kipa absolutely had to have a god, he would pick on something less unsavory than a five-inch black scorpion.

Kipa wanted Thurms to hold the squiggly little monster while he prepared the sand underfoot for the 'test.' But Thurms said *Gaagh!* and brushed it aside. So, nothing loath, Kipa tucked the struggling god into his garments.

"I'm going to call him Thoth after the Lord of Truth," he told Thurms. "Because he holds his tail upright as Thoth holds his symbol."

Down on hands and knees, Kipa smoothed a great circle of sand and traced upon it a fairly accurate map of Sinai. In the northern sector he made little ripples in the sand to represent the desert of Sinai. A yard below that he placed a line of pebbles and called them the Gebel Yelleq Range. Then he rooted the elusive Thoth from his clothes and placed him in the northwest corner of the sand map.

Thoth didn't want to do anything at first, except raise his tail and give something or someone a good wallop. Kipa gave him a nudge with a blunt forefinger and Thoth (rather reluctantly, Thurms thought) started out to explore the miniature desert.

He trekked due east into the Wilderness of Shur for about twelve inches, hesitated, then turned sharply south and started in the direction of the Great and Little Bitter Lakes. Midway he paused on a nameless stretch of desert—approximately where, Thurms knew, the Egyptians kept a small desert outpost, Fort Harba.

Suddenly Thoth took off in a rush, his four pairs of little feet clipping off the inches at a remarkable pace. He was traveling southeast, straight for the center of the row of pebbles. The Range.

Thoth's pair of pedipalpi, held out in front to test the terrain, came in contact with one of the pebbles and he grabbed at it with his pincers. This time he stopped for good, as though quite contented to remain right where he was.

Kipa raised a brightly inquiring, triumphant eye to Thurms.

Thurms didn't know what to say. He was a youthful product of a superstitious time. And an omen was an omen.

The aspect of the Daphnae garrison had suffered a change during Thurms' absence. There was the bustle of activity, the agitation of hurried preparations, and there were new faces. Thurms reported to headquarters and was greeted by a strange staff officer who appeared to be impatiently harassed.

"Thurms? Thurms?" he chanted distractedly. "Oh yes. You've been expected. The General asked after you."

"The General? Horemheb's here already? I have a dispatch for Commander Bek, telling of the General's coming—"

"Bek has been placed under arrest," the officer snapped. "The General didn't wait for the troop barges. He came on ahead by chariot and arrived yesterday."

"Bek under arrest?" Thurms was stunned. "Why, in Set's name?"

The staff officer had no time for such trivial matters. He shrugged it off, saying, "Something to do with dereliction of duty. I wouldn't know. The General's very wroth, very wroth indeed. Wait here . . ."

Thurms waited with nervous anticipation. He couldn't imagine how a seasoned veteran of Bek's caliber could find himself in hot water with the high command. Bek was the soldier who never made mistakes.

Horemheb received him in a hot buggy mud-walled room. It was crowded with staff officers and scribes; yet in any crowd, no matter how large, Horemheb would stand out like a wild hawk of trouble.

Head erect, blue eyes alight, he had the air of a man going into battle. His face, narrow and aquiline and stamped with experience and authority, had a look so nakedly ambitious it was alarming. It seemed to say, *Look out—I take! I never give.* Thurms felt somehow diminished under the General's luminous blue gaze.

"So, Thurms, son of Nefru!" he said in a voice that was meant to carry across battlefields. "You have the look of your father; *but*—" he jerked a grin like a grimace, "I understand that you have the habit of defying military tradition, of falling asleep on duty, and of losing all your equipment down to your sandals!"

Thurms wet his lips and opened his mouth to attempt a defense. But Horemheb wasn't waiting for one. He strode up and down the crowded room slapping at his thigh with the gold-braided whip of his office.

"Well, I've broken more military tradition in my day than King Menes broke Wa-shi heads in his. And I've dozed in the chariot in the thick of battle after three days and nights of combat and no sleep. And I've lost and scattered and thrown away more military equipment between here and Kush than there are stones in Cheops' pyramid! *But*—there is a right time to do these things and there is a *wrong* time!"

He stopped in mid-stride and grinned again, wolfishly.

"And your father the General seems to think you chose all the wrong times. Now—what was the great importance of this slave boy Kemheb?"

In detail, Thurms started to explain. But Horemheb was a soldier of such driving force that even the Egyptians themselves claimed they had never known his equal. He was not a daydreamer. He had no patience for the fanciful. If—in his youth—he had ever heard of Tenakertom, he had cast the legend aside as nonsense. He stopped Thurms with a scowl.

"By the left hind leg of Maut! Is that what soldiers think about here in the desert? Lost cities? Don't you fools realize we have a war to fight? Here I am in Ammon's garbage dump with sixty chariots and two thousand men, and Pharaoh expects me to daintily slap the wrists of ten thousand Khabiri savages and send them trundling home!

"And even when I arrive here what do I find? *Nothing!* No preparations, a half-asleep flea-bitten garrison with a motley handful of simple-minded soldiers who spend their time dreaming of lost cities! Set's sister! I don't even find the commander *on duty!* I find that he's been absent from his post for nearly two weeks!"

This seemed to remind him of something and he swung

to one of his officers to snap a terse order. "Fetch that fool Bek to me." He turned his hard blue eyes back to Thurms.

"Your father fears that you still don't know how to conduct yourself as a proper soldier. He has asked me to do something about you."

Thurms swallowed, with difficulty. Horemheb didn't elaborate on what he planned to 'do about' him. In fact, he seemed to have forgotten Thurms completely. He was perusing a map and muttering to himself over what he saw or didn't see there.

Bek, as belligerent-looking as ever, strode into the room and came to attention before the General. "Lord Horemheb, I protest about the highhanded treatment you have—"

"*You* protest!" Horemheb turned to him with fire in his eyes. "*I!* I protest, Bek. I protest every time I find a garrison commander absent without authority! Where in the name of Osiris' uncle have you been for two weeks?"

Bek's surly eyes blinked, somewhat taken aback by Horemheb's bombastic manner. "On desert duty," he replied readily enough, however. "Where did you think I'd be—in Thebes in the House of Death?"

"You might as well have been! Well—go on!"

Bek pulled at his battered nose. "I made an inspection tour out to Fort Harba." To which Horemheb turned, snatched up his map, and ran a finger rapidly across the surface.

"How long does it take to reach Harba—one day? How long does it take to inspect a two-by-four mud fort—one day? How long does it take to return from Harba—*twelve days?*"

"Well—" Bek fumbled, and glanced at Thurms. "Well, after the botch Thurms made of his patrol and the trouble he kicked up, I thought I had better do a little patrolling of my own. I'm responsible for this district, you know—"

"Never mind passing the blame to Thurms! He has problems enough of his own. A garrison commander isn't required to make personal patrols. By Horus, man, that's what you have patrol soldiers for! And the fact remains that you were absent from your post in a time of war . . . absent when I needed you most!"

Bek pulled up his squarish body with dignified defiance. "Very well, General. You're the great Set on wheels here. I have nothing more to say. I may assume that you are relieving me of my command?"

"You may wager your helmet on that!" Horemheb assured him. "I'm in charge here now. This will be my temporary headquarters until we can round up every available man and move toward the Khabiri."

Bek nodded. "I'm to remain under arrest, then?"

Horemheb's grimace-grin returned. "I don't think you heard me, Bek. I said 'every available man.' No no. You aren't going to sit around in some comfortable flea-popping mud hut wasting your time and mine."

He glanced at the map again. "You seem so fond of the desert around Harba that I'm putting you in charge of the fort out there."

Thurms glanced at Bek, almost with compassion. Fort Harba was considered to be the fag end of Set's backyard. It was nothing but fleas and sand and heat and sand and monotony and sand and dysentery and more sand. Soldiers frequently went mad out there.

But if Bek felt any of this, his tough soldier's face refused to show it. He gave no indication of emotion.

Suddenly Horemheb looked up and added—almost as an afterthought—"And Thurms will go as post adjutant."

Thoth, it seemed, must have had an off day. He hadn't brought Thurms the abundance of good luck that Kipa had promised he would.

7

FORT FLEA

I<small>T WAS</small> the same old desert with the same double tracks of the chariot wheels in the sands and with the usual hoof-tramplings in between. The illimitable desert where one saw the jackal, the hyena, the vulture, and the lizards. You never saw the sun, not directly; you never raised your head that high because sunblindness was not a pleasant thing to have.

But it was there, always, burning like the king of bonfires.

Thurms drove the chariot and Bek, as surly as a Ptah statue, stood behind him in a braced posture. They had very little to say to one another. It was a little like being on patrol with Hritut in the old days. Hritut . . . Thurms wondered what had become of him.

Moldering bones by now, he thought. *Somewhere in the hills beyond Azira's Well.* And Kipa was probably rending his garments to shreds (to Thoth's horror) in Daphnae because Bek had refused to take a civilian to Fort Harba.

Then, abruptly, he forgot about Hritut and Kipa as they came surging over the crest of a great dune and found themselves unwittingly charging down on a small band of Khabiri who were engaged in some industrious form of digging.

The Khabiri were obviously as startled and surprised to see the Egyptians as the Egyptians were to see the Khabiri. With cries of rage and terror the tribesmen scattered for their weapons; and it was then, as Thurms veered the team to the right, that he saw what the enemy was attempting to conceal in the sand. Jars, many many jars.

Bek was already nocking an arrow to a bow as he shouted:

"Further! Guide them further to the right! Get out of this!"

There were about a dozen Khabiri and Bek was probably right: the odds were against them. But Bek wasn't usually one to run from a fight, and his agitated insistence for escape puzzled Thurms; rather, it would have if he'd had time to think separate thoughts right then.

But his mind was on a single track.

He sawed the reins and swung the team back to the left, the Khabiri scrambling wildly now on all sides of them, and Bek simply roaring with shocked anger.

"Thurms! Are you out of your mind! *You're taking us into them!"*

Thurms knew it. He was doing it deliberately because there was something he had to find out for his own knowledge and satisfaction. The pile of half-buried jars was dead ahead now and he turned the team just slightly to catch one of the outside jugs with the off wheel.

There was a jolt and a crash and he looked back as the chariot swept on through the tumbling screaming Khabiri. The shards of the broken crock were lying in a dark liquid pool which was quickly being sucked down by the burning greedy sand.

Water. The enemy was burying jars of water in the desert.

Three of the Khabiri had gained the crest of a sand hill and they were drawing a careful bead on the two patrolmen with their wickedly barbed arrows, when a fourth—perhaps the leader—running along the foot of the dune, began screaming at them.

"*No! No!* The armlet! *The armlet,* you fools!"

The three archers lowered their bows and watched the wildly-careening chariot sweep by them with open-mouthed bewilderment.

Which was the same way that Bek and Thurms felt.

"Why didn't the pigs of Baal let loose at us?" Bek demanded. "They had us right where they wanted us—thanks to your idiocy!"

Thurms shook his head. He couldn't understand it either.

"I had to see what they had in those jars!" he called back.

"They could have cobra juice in there for all of me!"

"It means something—that water," Thurms insisted. "The Khabiri are stockpiling water jars at intervals across the desert for their soldiers and horses. Such a thing will place Horemheb at a worse disadvantage than ever!"

"May Sekhmet take Horemheb and drown him in the Eastern Sea!" Bek cried.

Thurms urged the team to put a greater expanse of sand between themselves and the Khabiri, and kept his mouth shut. Secretly he was puzzled by Bek's attitude. Bek didn't seem to be himself. He hadn't in the least minded his exile to the Set-hole of Fort Harba; he had most urgently wanted to run from a small fight; and he didn't seem to care a potter's wheel whether Horemheb lost the desert war or not.

He's changed somehow, Thurms thought. *But what exactly has brought on the change?*

The little fort sat in the boundless desert like an island in a sea. It was nudged up against a small oasis as though moored to the palms. Its block shape was enclosed within massive walls of sun-dried brick strengthened by longitudinal and transverse timbers. It had flanking towers on the four corners as well as a lookout tower over the gate. The walls had a slight incline and were crenellated at the top.

The lookout spotted the chariot coming and gave a shout. Quickly the soldiers gathered along the parapet, for any form of diversion—no matter how slight—was a welcome sight to the fifteen archers and the fifteen spearmen. They had been stuck in this nowhere post for two months and they needed excitement the way a drowning man needs a raft.

The gates were swung open and the chariot rolled through the oasis and into the fort and came to a halt on the small sandy square. Thurms looked up at the soldiers on the walls and made a snap decision about them. A bad lot, the incorrigible offsweepings of the army.

The commanding officer walked toward the chariot with the look of a man approaching an enemy rather than an ally.

"Back again, Bek?" he said sourly. "You must love us out here."

"About as much as you love me," Bek snapped. "I'm taking command. Horemheb is in Daphnae."

"What about our relief?" a sergeant yelled down from the wall.

Bek snorted. "You'll be relieved when that wolf of Asyut Horemheb says you'll be relieved—which will probably be sometime in the 20th Dynasty." Bek turned back to the officer. "Senmut, this is Thurms, a general's son. He's our adjutant."

"He's welcome to it," was all Senmut had to say.

Bek, Senmut, and Thurms sat around a rough plank table in the small stifling officers' quarters and drank Syrian red wine liberally laced with water. Bek tasted it and spat on the floor. "By Anubis' eye-tooth! Why don't you just drink water instead?"

Senmut made a noise in his throat. "We think the spring in the oasis is going bad. So we try to cut down the dysentery with wine."

His face was molded on delicate bones, with a wide smooth forehead and hollowed temples. He had a bland stoical look, yet little shadows and contractions were continually in play around his red-rimmed eyes and weak mouth. Thurms realized there was something wrong with the man, but he couldn't pinpoint the trouble.

"How is the dysentery?" he asked.

"Three down with it, four just getting over it. Two buried."

"How have the Khabiri been?"

"Not bad. We haven't had a brush with them in a week. I think something's building, though. We see them passing everyday."

Thurms nodded and turned to Bek, who didn't seem to be paying much attention to the conversation. "We should send a messenger to Daphnae at once, sir. Horemheb should know about those Khabiri water deposits."

Bek looked at him blankly for a moment, then grunted. "Very well. I'll send a runner."

Thurms and Senmut both gave the CO a startled look. "Runner?" Thurms echoed. "You mean a man on foot? Why not send the chariot?"

Bek didn't seem to want to talk about it. He stood up and spoke over his shoulder as he headed for the door. "Because it's the only chariot and team we have. Allow *me* to worry about it, will you? I'm running things here."

Thurms looked at Senmut. The officer's petulant mouth made a down-cornered smile.

"You didn't really think he'd turn his chariot loose, did you?"

"Why not, for Set's sake?" Thurms demanded. "He has

military information that should reach Horemheb just as quickly as possible."

Senmut sneered. "You don't know Bek."

"That's what I am beginning to suspect. He told Horemheb that he was out here for two weeks on an inspection tour. What was he really up to?"

Senmut laughed without humor. "He has more lies in him than Anubis has teeth. He was here, but he didn't stay. He came and he went. One time he'd be gone for two days; then he'd return for food and water. Next time he'd be gone for four days, and so on."

"But what was he doing? What was his purpose?"

Senmut slouched back into his chair and into a brooding mood.

"How would I know?"

The wisp of an idea dragged across Thurms' brain and he leaned over the table tensely.

"Senmut—what direction would he take?"

"The same one every time. Southeast. Straight for the Range."

When Thurms stepped out into the white explosion of sun in the square he thought that he must have developed sunstroke. The air was thick with fleet-moving little specks that made everything look off-focus, as though the beholder were suffering from vertigo. The very walls of the fort seemed to be in some amazing process of continuous, yet static disintegration. Dizzily, Thurms made fists of his hands and scrubbed at his eyes. When he looked again he saw that the air around him was still cracking with the mysterious specks.

"By Set's scepter!" he cried at a passing, scratching spearman. "What is happening to the air? What is that I see—or think I see?"

The soldier grinned at him. "Fleas. Didn't you know? Every time there's a lot of movement around the fort they come up from the sand. Your chariot disturbed them this time."

Thurms looked at his bare arms. They were covered with black vermin, popping on and off.

"Do you have to live like this all the time?" he cried.

"You've seen nothing," the soldier assured him. "Wait until you have dysentery and fleas and we have a real heat wave and the Khabiri attack us—everything at once. Then you'll see some desert madness!"

The desert madness was a common curse among outpost soldiers. The one thing in its favor was that it usually was not a long-lasting ailment. But while it had a man in its wild clutch it could prove to be very dangerous. Soldiers so afflicted might run amok, kill their officers or own comrades or even themselves.

It was brought on mostly by the grueling never-ending monotony of outpost life, with the generous help of frustration, heat, discipline, sand fleas, dust, fever, and a brain-numbing sense of depression that comes from loneliness.

On Thurms' first night in the fort one of the soldiers suddenly went mad and rushed through the gate to the edge of the oasis, tore off all his clothes and began to dance naked in the ghostly Sinai moonlight, with a dagger in his hand.

Thurms found the soldiers standing along the parapet watching, and Senmut in the gateway doing the same thing. No one seemed too concerned about the madman dancing naked in the moonlight.

"Aren't you going to do anything?" Thurms wondered.

Senmut shrugged. "There are only three possibilities. One, we shoot an arrow into him from a safe distance. Two, we wait until he accidentally or deliberately kills himself with the knife. And three, we wait until he finally wears himself out and collapses."

"But the second possibility might occur at any moment!"

"Surely," Senmut agreed.

"Then why don't we attempt to capture him before he hurts himself?"

"With that knife in his hand?" Senmut shuddered at the thought.

Scowling, and with some trepidation, Thurms walked out through the black and silver crisscross of the oasis shadows and paused by the bole of a gaunt old palm to study the situation.

The madman was dancing solemnly on a sparse patch of turf at the foot of the outer palms. The dagger in his hand looked very long and the moon sparked on the blade and ran down it like quicksilver.

Thurms stepped out of the shadows and started around to the left, getting into the sand. Instantly the madman spotted him and ceased his whirling antics. He crouched low, as though ready to leap. Thurms smiled in the moonlight and held out his hand.

"Let me be your friend."

The madman didn't want a friend. He wanted an enemy. "Khabiri!" he hissed at Thurms. Nor could he be persuaded that he was wrong in holding to his erroneous belief. "Khabiri!" he insisted, and he made a tentative pass in the air at Thurms with the dagger.

Thurms decided to adopt a new strategy. He dropped to his knees in the sand, facing the demented man.

"Yes, I'm a Khabiri. Look out for yourself, I'm creeping up on you." He put his hand down on the sand in front of him.

The madman made a guttural sound in his throat and came at him in a wild bound. Thurms scooped up a handful of sand, tossed it into the on-coming distorted face, rolled left and stuck out his right leg. Blinded, the madman clipped over Thurms' leg and went into a somersault landing flat on his back in an eagle-spread, as Thurms shoved up and launched himself for the outflung arm and the dagger.

Pitching the weapon into the sands, he straddled the struggling man's chest and pinned him there. Then he gave a call to the fort.

"Senmut! Send some men with a rope!"

Later, in his own little ovenlike cubbyhole which contained his cot and personal equipment, Thurms received the dour-visaged Senmut.

"That was very foolish of you, Thurms," Senmut complained. "What do you think would happen to me if I had to report the death of a general's son—who was under my command?"

"Something had to be done for the poor fellow, and no one else seemed willing to do it," Thurms replied. "Will he be all right?"

"Yes yes, that sort of ailment always passes within a few days. But I still maintain—"

"Listen, Senmut. Don't be too concerned over the fact that I'm the son of a general. A general's son must expect death the same as any soldier. Besides, I'm under Bek's command. Not yours."

Senmut gave a nervous mirthless laugh. "That shows how much you know. You and I are the only officers left in Harba."

Thurms looked at him blankly. "I don't understand."

"Quite simple—Bek's gone again. Ran off with the team and chariot while the men were securing the madman in the lazarette."

8

THE SANDS OF SET

THE DAWN UNCOVERED a grim spectacle for Fort Flea. The lookout called Thurms and Senmut to the main wall and pointed into the quiet oasis. At first Thurms saw nothing except palms, shaded sand, and the little well. Then he realized that one of the palms bore strange fruit.

Bek's runner was hanging by his heels from the tree. Dead, very dead.

Thurms swallowed and waited nervously for Senmut's orders. But Senmut seemed to be in a kind of mental funk. He stared at the dead soldier fixedly. Finally Thurms ventured to say:

"Shall I order some men out to bring in the body?"

Senmut gave a start and turned to him with his face atwitch.

"Out there? Send men out there? Are you insane? Can't you see the oasis is acrawl with skulking Khabiri?"

Thurms looked again and he still saw the palms, the sand, and the well. That was all.

"Senmut, there's no one out there—no one who is alive, at least."

Senmut wiped his moist face with a trembling hand. He looked at the oasis suspiciously and became silent again. Thurms waited uneasily for an order, any order. But Senmut remained mute.

"Shall I double the guard?" Thurms offered hopefully.

"The guard? Why? You said there were no Khabiri out there."

Thurms let out his breath quietly. "Not in the oasis. But the presence of that dead man means that the Khabiri are close by—out in the sands, behind the dunes. They're obviously up to something."

Senmut became peevishly excited. "How do you know that? How do you know they're up to something? Who told you that?"

Thurms looked at the senior officer dubiously. Then, gently, he took him by the elbow. "Senmut, why don't you go to your quarters and take a little rest? Get out of this accursed sun for a bit."

Senmut nodded distractedly, the subtle facial contractions playing over his eyes and mouth. "Yes, yes . . . that's what I'll do. I—I'm not feeling well . . . a touch of sun perhaps. You take care of things, Thurms. You take charge . . ." He wandered away rather dazedly.

Thurms rubbed at the back of his neck and went to work. He changed the guard in the tower and doubled the guard on the four walls. He ordered the gates open and sent out a detail to bring in a reserve supply of water, and another smaller detail to fetch in the dead man. Then he sent half of his command to breakfast. A sergeant brought him a clay tablet, saying:

"It was at the foot of the palm where Metufer was hanging."

We are 400 to your 30. Will you capitulate? Or by the 40 baboons of Osiris we will overrun you!

Thurms handed the tablet back to the sergeant, ordering him to take it to the top of the tower, break it, and toss the pieces into the oasis. After that he went to Senmut's quarters to see how the senior officer was getting on.

Senmut was not 'getting on' at all—at least not in a very normal fashion. Thurms found him hiding under his bed.

"Senmut, what are you doing under there?"

"Go away! Go away! I'm looking for my god."

"Your god?"

"Yes yes! I have a stone scarab which is a very valuable god. I cannot find him anywhere! Where is he? I must have him!"

"I'm sure I don't know where he is," Thurms said patiently. "But if you'll come out from under the bed I'll help you look for him."

Senmut didn't want to come out from under the bed. He said he would stay there forever until his scarab was brought to him. And he said that he knew it *couldn't* be brought to him because that son of Set, Bek, had run off with it.

"Why would Bek want to do such a thing, Senmut?"

"Because he hates me!" Senmut cried in a childish rage. "Because he knows I will die in battle without my scarab to protect me, and he knows the Khabiri are about to attack us at any moment!"

Thurms was appalled by the realization that Senmut had finally succumbed to the desert madness. He sat on a stool and looked bleakly at Senmut, who peered out at him from under the edge of the bed.

Bek gone, Senmut mad, a small half-crazed, half-sick garrison holding a fort full of fleas against an imminent Khabiri attack. And Thurms was now in command.

When it came it was all at once and without a hint of warning. One moment the white desert lay empty and the blue sky spread silent; the next moment Set, the god of war, was in the sands of Sinai and the desert was acrawl with running Khabiri and the sky aquiver with their horrifying war cries.

Ul-ul-ul-ul-ul-ullah! The screams rolled toward the little fort like an advancing sea. The Egyptians responded with horns, blowing—*Traaadooon! Traaadooon!* and everyone rushed for the parapets, grabbing up helmets and bows and quivers of arrows and javelins.

Thurms snatched for his helmet and ran from his quarters and up the ramp to the east wall. All across the rolling dunes he saw the Khabiri coming, hundreds of them, swinging around the fort in a quickly closing circle. Their spear-blades flashed in the sun, and already their arrows were winging sleekly toward the crenellated walls.

"By the false beard of Pharaoh!" a burly sergeant cried. "Chariots! They've got war chariots! Where could they have found them?"

"From the Egyptian garrisons in Syria, you fool!" Thurms yelled. "Get your squad in order. I want a seven-man squad on each wall. That leaves one man for the tower and one for—"

"That leaves no one," the sergeant corrected him. "Metufer's dead, and Mata's still locked in the lazarette as mad as a crocodile with a stake between its jaws!"

And another subtraction was quickly made. The Khabiri who were rapidly infiltrating the oasis found the lookout in the tower to be an irresistible target and they saluted him with a dark flight of arrows. The lookout disappeared behind his little square of battlements with a gurgled cry. Thurms decided against sending another man up there to take his place. The position was too exposed.

The Egyptian bowstrings went *twa-twa-twa-twang* all around the walls and here, there, near and far robe-clad

Khabiris toppled over and sprawled like lifeless sacks on the sand.

But the returning arrow fire was something to marvel at. From behind every dune, every palm trunk and from the elevated shelter of the palms' shaggy heads, and from the racing chariots a murderous rain of arrows whickered up, down, over and into the fort. They came with a *wwwunch-wwwunch* through the murmuring air, striking walls and woodwork and helmets and copper-tabbed corselets and men.

Thurms saw a soldier stagger back from his place at the wall, a brightly feathered stylus-thin shaft jutting from his chest, and topple headlong off the parapet and into the sand of the enclosure.

"Spread your squads!" Thurms shouted. "Keep your intervals even along the walls!" And he had a fearful inkling that very shortly those intervals were going to become wider and wider.

The rolling, sand-spinning chariots were swinging closer and closer to the walls, heedless of their own foot soldiers and their dead and wounded. The Egyptian bows went *twatwatwa-twammm!* at them, and charioteers would throw up their hands and fall back on the reins as the frantic teams would take off on erratic courses of their own, the wildly careening chariots bouncing behind.

Each chariot carried a three-man crew: charioteer, fighter, and sling man. The sling men twirled long slings over their heads as the chariots passed close under the walls and when they released them a small jar of flaming oil would come spinning upward and land with a splash of flame and the spewing liquid fire was deadly to man and woodwork alike.

Thurms had to take three men away from the walls and set them to firefighting.

Now streamers of white smoke rose from the fort mingling

with the vaster shimmer of the desert's heat haze, while the arrows and javelins and spears hummed downward and winged upward and the flame jars went *plowm! plowm!* against the sun-baked bricks, as the chariots clattered and spun in the sand and the Khabiri archers somersaulted earthward out of the palm trees, and the Egyptians dropped their weapons and started to step away from them and lost their sense of direction and purpose and fell from the parapets helplessly.

Then the attackers pulled back and a great silence smothered over the fort, and soldiers dropped right where they were and put their moist faces in their grimy hands and for long moments they wouldn't move at all, or speak.

Thurms counted heads and discovered that he had lost nine men. He also discovered that the fool firefighters had used the drinking water to quench the numerous little fires that had broken out during the fighting. He gave these men a severe dressing down and sent for his sergeants. They didn't look happy at all. They said one more attack like the first one and they might as well throw their hands in the air and consider themselves dead.

"Have you lost your reason?" Thurms admonished them. "We still have food and water and weapons and twenty men. Hasn't anyone ever told you that while there's life there's hope?"

Presumably no one ever had, until now, and even after they heard the axiom they didn't care to put much stock in it. Annoyed, Thurms ordered them back to duty. He sent half the garrison down to the barracks to eat and rest, and kept the other half on the walls. Then he went to see how Senmut was doing.

Senmut was doing the same thing as before: hiding under his bed. Thurms left him there because it seemed as safe a place to be in the little fort as any other.

It seemed to him that he had no sooner thrown himself on his hot cot to toss and doze fitfully when the horns began to blow again.

Traaadooon! Traaadooon!

Muttering curses about Set and his sister and uncle and other assorted relatives, he hurried up to the west wall. The soldiers were yelling, "They're coming! They're coming!" And from out of the shadowy moon-struck desert rolled the *Ul-ul-ul-ul-ullah!* of the attackers' throaty war cry.

From the parapet the desert looked flat and gray in the moonlight. Barely discernible were the black buglike shapes of the chariots scuttling toward the fort. Thurms ordered the men to prepare firebrands. "Wait until the chariots are within fifty yards of the walls," he told the sergeants. "Then pitch the torches over so that our men may see their targets. Tell them not to waste arrows on the teams. The horses are too well protected. Concentrate on the charioteers!"

The chariots came clattering in with the multiple pound of hoofs, and Thurms shouted *NOW!* and all around the walls the firebrands went twisting end over end like spinning Catherine wheels and plopped and flared in the sand, creating many little islands of orange light.

The chariots flicker-spoked through the little bundles of flame, and pale dabs of swift-moving faces looked up at the battlements as the bowstrings snapped *twam-twam-twam!* at them. The slings twirled over the charioteers' heads and the little jars of flaming oil described vivid parabolas across the night sky.

Thurms set his firefighters to work again and they had their hands full. Within minutes the fort had taken on a festive, militant aspect, with dozens of crackling and radiant fanions fluttering above the walls. The flames rose resplendent into the desert night.

By the clepsydra, the water clock, the fight lasted an hour.

Then the Khabiri tide receded into the dark sand hills, drawing further and further off with ever-diminishing cries of a threatening nature. Thurms received the reports from his noncoms (four casualties, all fires under control), and mounted the guard and secured the fort for the night.

Bone weary, harassed beyond belief, and (secretly) frightened, he staggered to his quarters and back to his cot. He was beginning to believe that Kemheb had known what he was talking about. War was not a true adventure. It was a substitute for personal achievement.

The sun, having scuttled under the flat bottom of the earth (so everyone believed), peeked over the eastern lip like a brightly inquiring eye, to see the Khabiri return with the dawn. This time there was no respite between sunrise and sunset. They came pouring through the oasis with their spears, they crowded along the dunes with their showers of arrows, they ringed the fort in with their rampantly rolling chariots, slinging up their flaming jars.

The melting African sun stood dead above and baked the desert fort like a griddlecake. The soldiers cried for water in husky voices, and the sand fleas simply had a heyday, snapping and popping and criss-crossing the troubled air until it was hard to take and hold a correct sight on a target and many arrows went wide of their mark by yards.

You had to give the Khabiri credit, Thurms conceded ruefully. They were great ones for making use of what few materials they had on hand to further their attack. They started slinging in jars which neither smoked nor flamed.

The first jar landed on the north parapet with a *pow!* and Thurms and his men were horrified to see a ghastly tangle of venomous snakes come hissing and wiggling from the shards. The serpents zigzagged off in every direction at once, snapping at everything that moved.

It was now every man for himself. You squinted your eyes against the sun glare and sweat and flickering fleas, and shot an arrow at a Khabiri who wouldn't remain stationary, and you looked down and chopped at an angry snake underfoot, and you dodged around a pool of liquid fire and hacked a few more snakes out of your way and took up a new position along the parapet and twanged off another arrow . . .

Thurms turned with a look of desperation and counted the men still on their feet. Two, crouching and firing and shifting along the west parapet; two more on the north; three fighting on the east; and himself alone on the south wall. Eight men.

The fight dragged on and on. So did the sun.

Six men.

Five.

An archer, half blind with fatigue, sun and heat, stumbled against Thurms on the south wall. They looked at each other bleakly, the wailing, coming *Ul-ul-ul-ul-ullah!* rising all around them.

"We're lost if they swarm the walls," the archer said. "And why haven't they? What in Maut's name has been holding them back?"

Thurms shook his head. "I don't know. Keep moving. Make them think we're still able to man our battlements."

Four men.

Three.

Then . . .

The burning sun settled slowly, lazily over its western chamber and began to smolder on the far-away dunes. Broad, swift gray fingers of twilight stretched toward the fort and oasis. Thurms, standing alone and haggard on the dead-littered, weapon-cluttered west parapet, lowered his empty bow and looked around at the vacant walls.

He was quite alone. Even the snakes were dead.

Curiously, the oasis and surrounding dunes were very still; no clattering chariot wheels or sand-pounding hoofs, no *thumm* of bowstrings or *wwunch* of speeding arrows, no war cries. Silence.

For one moment hopelessness swept over him and he was almost lost in a deep well of despair indescribable. But he perked up and shucked the mood like a pair of worn-out sandals. He was young, a soldier, he was a general's son. It went against his nature simply to give up.

He went to work industriously, gathering up a great armload of small faggots from the woodshed, spacing them in little piles at equal intervals around the parapets. Then, satisfied for the moment, and with night not yet firmly entrenched, he went below again and into Senmut's quarters.

Senmut was still playing turtle under his cot, but he

seemed much calmer than before. He peered anxiously up at Thurms.

"Have the Khabiri gone?"

"I think so," Thurms lied. He saw no sense in setting Senmut off again. "How are you feeling?"

"Feeling? Feeling? I feel fine. Why shouldn't I feel fine? If—if I only had my scarab, though." His face glowered with sudden consuming anger. "That Bek! That thrice accursed dog! Stealing my god!"

"Why do you think he would do such a thing?" Thurms asked to pacify the unhappy, unsettled man.

A sly look came into Senmut's wavering eyes. "Because he's looking for something out there, and he took my scarab for luck. He can't fool me. He's on to something, and it has nothing to do with war."

It was remarkable, Thurms reflected, that men whom other men judge insane frequently have deeper, truer insight to the heart of a matter than their judges. Because there was no doubt in Thurms' mind (nor had there been for some time now) that Bek had been bitten by the gold bug of Tenakertom.

A sudden shout from outside snapped him from his reverie.

"Hail the fort! Is anyone alive in there?"

From the north parapet Thurms could see a suggestion of movement among the shadowy black-trunk palms down in the oasis. He nocked an arrow in his bow and waited.

"Curs of Egypt! Can you answer?" a voice cried out, teasing Thurms' memory with a ring of familiarity.

"We can answer, lice of the desert!" he shouted back.

There was a pause, and then a sudden small blare of light, and a torch was tossed among the palms to a clear patch in the sand. With caution, a palm frond was stretched toward the halo of light and waved to and fro. The universal symbol of peace: to the military world—a flag of truce.

"Will you honor the palm frond?" the voice inquired hopefully.

"Certainly. We are not barbarians here."

A short fat robed figure stepped into the little circle of light. The distance was too great to distinguish his features.

"Is the General's son still alive?" the man called with a trace of urgency in his voice. Thurms started. It was a most unexpected question.

"I am Thurms, the General's son. Who are you?"

"Thurms!" the fat man cried ecstatically. "Ammon's benevolence passes belief! I feared that these jackal-brained fools might have unwittingly killed you. It is I, your devoted friend, Azmachis!"

Azmachis! By the masons' stone-rockers, Thurms marveled, the ways of the gods were truly strange ways. But he kept his surprise well concealed from his 'devoted friend.'

"State your business, doghead, before my impatient men puncture your barrel belly with their arrows." He thought he caught a chuckle from Azmachis.

"Your *men*, mighty warrior of Kem? Can dead men draw bowstrings? I feel I have little to fear from your fort of dead."

Mighty warrior of Kem . . . that was who had first addressed him so: Azmachis. Thurms looked down at the jackal-head armlet he was wearing. Its mysterious owner had approached him with the same salutation.

"I said state your business. My men are my concern."

"True, true," Azmachis hastened to agree. "Will you open your gates for me, that we might converse in a more social and private—"

"No!" This time he distinctly heard Azmachis chuckle.

"Trying to keep your dead men a secret from me, eh Thurms? Crafty rogue you!"

"Azmachis," Thurms said loftily, "I am hungry and my evening meal awaits. Will you speak, or shall I give the order to have a burning beaker of oil upended over you?"

"Very well, Thurms. You know exactly what I wish to hear from you! Where is that scurvy son of a son of a son of a slave—Kemheb?"

"How should I know? Am I his keeper? He ran away from me at Azira's Well."

"Lies! Lies!" Azmachis cried wrathfully. "You would never let him go—knowing the precious secret he held!"

"His secrets are his own. And I did not let him go. He took my chariot and ran off while I was asleep."

"Ah-ha! And we know toward *where* and to *what* he ran, do we not, Thurms, eh? eh?"

"We do not," Thurms replied frostily. "He could have run to Set and all his devils for all I care or know."

Azmachis was beside himself with frustrated rage. He clawed his garments to rags. He threw himself down and poured sand in his hair. He yanked at his beard until it became evident to him that the hairy tangle wouldn't leave his face.

"False Egyptian! Greedy lying thieving offcast of Thebes' gutters! You *do* know where he has gone! And more—you know how to follow him! He confided in you! He told you! He gave you the Key! He—"

Azmachis had to pause to let his lungs pant about for some air. Then, with great difficulty, he calmed himself and pointed a resolved finger up at Thurms.

"I am giving you your last chance, Thurms. Confide in me, or I'll have my tribesmen overrun your dice box of a fort as though they were delta ants swarming over a sweetmeat!"

Thurms wet his lips and swallowed. "Let them come on," he said with false bravado. "My eager soldiers are waiting for them."

"The lie of lies!" Azmachis wailed. "You command a garrison of *dead men!* You cannot possibly have more than a handful yet on their feet! I give you five at the most!"

"Snake of Sinai!" Thurms shouted. "Your rantings bore me, and your swine-toned voice is annoying to the ears of my men—who now await my order to start their evening meal!"

He turned and ducked down to snatch up a brand from a fire bucket, calling out in a loud, carrying voice to his dead fort, "Start your cookfires! We will waste no more time listening to that prating fool!"

Quickly he went around the parapets, touching each small, combustible pile of faggots with the torch, his crouching silhouette leaping always just in front of a fresh fat spearblade of flame, until he had completed the round and stood at last in a corner of the square of fire. He rather imagined that the evenly spaced little cluster of fires had, from a reasonable distance, the aspect of an orderly military encampment. Cookfires . . . that would never warm the rations of the soldiers who would never again need them.

Would the ruse work? He honestly doubted it. Azmachis was too shrewd a man to be taken in by such a feeble trick. It was, admittedly, only a poor stall for time—though for what end (other than an unpleasant one) he did not know.

He gathered together a bundle of javelins, three quivers of arrows, his sword and bow, some food and water, and went up to the lookout tower, armed and prepared and resolved for the last stand.

But it didn't come.

He paced the close black walls. He studied the dark silent motionless desert. He went below and fed his cookfires fresh faggots, and checked the water clock. One liquid hour drained after another. And still—nothing.

He returned to the tower and sat down, his back in the northwest salient angle, and tried to keep his eyes open and his senses alert. Slowly, painlessly, the untended cookfires burned down down down to embers and smoldered out. Thurms dozed.

Noiselessly, dawn smashed over the eastern dunes, and for a long static moment the world seemed to hold its breath. Then a huge wheel of history came rolling out of the northern horizon and thundered down on the little fort that crouched against the Harba Oasis.

Thurms, stupid with sleep, helmetless, short hair on end, stood at the wall and gaped at the mightiest, unruliest army he had ever imagined, coming helter skelter across the sands.

The savage Khabiri army.

9

THE WHITE CIRCLE

THEY CAME by the thousands: ten thousand would have been any observer's shortest guess. They came on foot, running, they came on chariots and ox sleds and pack asses. Rapidly the landscape evolved itself into struggling knots of beasts and men; little clusters of horses and great swarming festers of men, whipping manes and tails, spearblades and sword-points catching the first sparks of the peacock-colored dawn.

A great medley of yells and horse sounds rose from the din of feet and hoofs and wheels. Thurms watched them pour across the yellow glades of sunlight which tilted toward the crests of the dunes, and even as he stood there awestruck—expecting at any moment to be overrun by this mighty host—the ragged head of the disorderly army wrenched away from the oasis and veered straight east.

Utterly bewildered he watched the savage army flow like a colorful river past the oasis, the butchered air insane with noise and dust and flashings of light. Rocking, jolting, thumping and rolling, the swarm churned by Harba and disappeared at last over the eastern dunes, leaving behind the billowing dust banners of their frantic passage.

Thurms wiped at his mouth, at his eyes. He caught his breath and turned to the north again. More of them were coming! He could see their pillowy dust cloud, blowing like Set's wrathful breath.

This second group was much smaller than its predecessor, and more orderly in its alignment and movements. A squadron of chariots formed the spearhead, and—he looked again —the chariots were bearing standards showing the bronze figures of the hawks of Hierakonpolis and Idfu and the wolf of Asyut and the cow head of Hathor.

Egyptians! Horemheb's army had the Khabiri on the run!

By the time Horemheb came bouncing into the oasis in his great war chariot, his staff officers had already entered the battered fort and learned of its grim tale from Thurms. They, in turn, had imparted their news of recent developments to him, and it would appear that he had taken another unwitting step into hot water.

Horemheb's army had started into the desert two days ago. On the previous evening they had collided with the Khabiri vanguard, which they had whipped soundly and put to rout. This beaten spearhead had turned back on its own advancing army in great agitation and disorder, creating a special panic which every soldier is subject to and which every general fears worse than death.

Confused, incapable of reason, panic-stricken and caught in the screaming chaos of dark, the Khabiri army had spooked like a herd of horses and had taken off en masse in a hysteria of haste.

Horemheb, shrewd in the ways and fortunes of war, realizing that by pure accident he suddenly had the Khabiri on the run, was quick to follow up his advantage. He set his army to the chase, intent on herding the Khabiri into the boxlike trap of the Great and Little Bitter Lakes in the south.

Then—two hours before dawn—the advantage slipped from his grasp.

The fleeing Khabiri army had spotted the glow of a fire, or many fires, in the southeast; and thinking (and, as the case was, rightly) that the fires could only be caused by other Khabiri, they had veered in that direction, swept up to the little fort at dawn, met with Azmachis' tribesmen, and all together had charged on into the desert of Sinai—where Horemheb could not hope to trap them.

Wonder of wonders! Kipa, as rotund and bald and sweaty as ever, came chuff-chuffing breathlessly into the fort and threw his arms wide to express his unbounded joy at finding Thurms alive and well.

"Aton and Ammon and all the rest be praised! I have found my master!" he cried and threw himself on the ground to wallow in the sand.

"Get up from there this instant!" Thurms was understandably embarrassed by the grins and chuckles of the onlooking staff officers.

"Kipa, you rogue. What are you doing here with the army?"

Kipa got up brushing sand from his face. "What am I doing here? What am I doing here?" he cried. "I am here because *you* are here! Is not a servant's place with his master? Is not a master without a servant no master at all? Is not a servant without a master no—"

Thurms gave him a good shake. "Stop that fork-tongued nonsense and answer me! What are you doing here with the army?"

Kipa put his finger to the side of his nose slyly.

"When I heard that that illustrious General of generals

was ready to move against the Khabiri, I volunteered my services as an oxdriver. First, because it is the duty of every Egyptian to serve his country unflinchingly during time of war; and second, because I was certain that sooner or later I would find my master out here in this pest hole, to whom I have pledged my eternal devotion, and who means more to me than my own immortality when I finally abandon my earthly body and step into Ammon's golden boat and drift across the azure sky—"

"Yes yes," Thurms said impatiently. He had a fairly accurate idea of Kipa's boundless devotion and love. Kipa was devoted to helping Thurms find Tenakertom for the love of lost treasure.

Horemheb strode through the gateway wearing a thundercloud for an expression. He slapped his gold-braid whip against his naked thigh and fastened his hard blue eyes on Thurms.

"Well, Thurms, still alive?" He didn't seem overly pleased about it. "You must be the possessor of an amulet of luck that beggars description. I understand that I have you to thank for turning the Khabiri rabble off the course I had intended for them."

"Well, sir—" Thurms began, fumblingly.

"We will say no more about it," Horemheb said crisply. "Fortunes of war." But from the look he gave Thurms, Thurms felt that the General was going to *think* quite a bit more about it. *Truly,* he thought, *with the luck I have had with generals, I will never make my way in the army.*

Horemheb glanced around at the parapets. "All dead, eh?"

"No sir," Thurms reported. "There are two men recovering from the desert madness. The commander is one of them."

Horemheb shot an eyebrow. "That desert rat Bek is still alive?"

"I don't mean Bek, sir. Senmut. Bek left the first night."

Horemheb's brows leveled to match the grim line of his mouth.

"Are you saying he deserted his post *again?* By Horus' hawk cap! Was there ever such a soldier!" He paused and gave Thurms a penetrating look. "Do you have any idea why this misguided fool keeps running off into the desert by himself?"

"Yes sir. I believe I do."

"Well? Well?"

"I believe that ever since I first told him of what I had heard of Tenakertom, he has been searching for it."

"Tenakertom!" Horemheb roared. "That child's fancy again! Can't anyone in this flea-mad land of sand think of anything except Tenakertom? Only let me set my hands on Bek and I'll tenakertom him into the House of Death!" He turned away, pivoting on one heel, and pointed his whip of office at the walls of the fort.

"Clean up this mess! I'm making this flea-trap my temporary headquarters. I'll expect all staff and field officers in the oasis for a council of war in ten drips of the clepsydra. We must formulate an immediate method of procedure against the Khabiri."

His officers and aides and scribes scattering like bees out of an overturned hive, Horemheb started to stride away—only to stop short and to cock the one significant eyebrow back at Thurms.

"It will probably be a while before we come into grip with the enemy again—thanks to you, Thurms. And I see no reason why you should simply stand around like a standard driven into the sand."

"Yes—er no, sir," Thurms said hesitantly.

"We must find a little duty for you; a little chore of a military nature," Horemheb mused.

"Yes sir," Thurms said, apprehensively.

"Let me see now . . . I was almost overlooking Bek, wasn't I? He's an army deserter, and it is up to the army to find him and bring him back to a court-martial, isn't it?"

"I—I believe so, sir."

"Well, then why are you standing there!" Horemheb roared. "And take that bag of fat with you before I have him melted down and served to my men for butter!"

Kipa scuttled fearfully after Thurms.

So it hadn't been left up to him after all. Truly the gods worked in mysterious ways. From that first day when he had met Kemheb and heard of Tenakertom the gods had been slowly but inexorably pushing him in the trackless direction of the lost city. He had felt it more and more, with each passing day. And now—miraculously—he practically had authorized orders to go and find it.

For miles, for a day and a night and a day they followed a chain of oases southeast, bumping and clattering in a doubtful old chariot drawn by a sorry old team—the best Horemheb could afford to release from his little army.

Veiled, cloaked men they saw, from the strange vast land to the south, and scatterings of Khabiri on foot, whom they outran, and drifts of so-called peaceful Sinai tribesmen. Not peaceful enough, however, for Thurms' and Kipa's liking.

They had made a halt at one of the lonely little oases, watered the team and fed themselves, and were returning to the well to replenish their waterskins when they suddenly found themselves blocked off from the chariot by eight or nine tribesmen.

"Greetings, brothers!" Thurms said hopefully, Kipa clinging hesitantly to his elbow. "Aton bless you."

"Try Ammon," Kipa suggested in a whisper, when the flint-eyed men remained mute and unmoved. "Or perhaps Baal. He's the Syrian god."

The tribesmen gathered slowly around, hemming them in, silently at first. Then Thurms detected a muttering undertone: *"Roumis—Roumis,"* and he noticed that all of them were armed with short curved-bladed swords. Their hostile intent was obvious.

His hand flinched toward his sword, and with that one tentative movement a deeply menacing growl issued from the tribesmen's throats like the rumbling threat of an advancing sea.

It was a bad moment: death, as sure as Pharaoh's taxes, was crowding them. Bitterly, Thurms remembered Horemheb's jocular reference about his possession of an amulet of luck that beggared description, and he wished that it were true. Luck was about the only thing that could save them. Even wiggly old Thoth seemed to have let them down.

They took a hesitant step backwards . . . the tribesmen pressed in. Then Thurms thought, *Amulet—armlet.* Carefully, he reached for his right arm and removed the jackal-head armlet, glancing at the ring of intent dark faces. The tribesmen were watching the curious armlet with avid attention.

With a snap of his arm Thurms lobbed the coil of gold high into the air and to the left, yelling, "It belongs to he who is first!"

Automatically the cluster of men broke into a shouting scramble for the prize, and Thurms and Kipa went for the chariot at a run—Thurms leaping to the platform and snatching for the reins and yelling *YAH!* bolting the team from a deadstart, and Kipa running and cursing and clutching at the back struts of the basket-weave.

"Wait! Wait! Foul inconsiderate master!"

Thurms reached around and caught Kipa by the scruff of his grimy neckband and pulled him up like a sack of grain. Now that Kipa was safely in the chariot and out of the clutch of the hostile tribesmen his bravado and accusations and advice were remarkable to hear.

"You threw away a small fortune in that armlet! You should never have used such extreme means to extricate us from such a minor predicament! You should have let *me* handle the situation. I could have dazzled their simple minds with feats of magic! I could have stunned their sensibilities by reading the sands for them! I could have mystified them, and sooth-ed them, and—"

"And close your mouth!" Thurms ordered. "You couldn't sooth which way a river was running if you were standing in it. That armlet has served a worthy purpose which Azmachis never intended it for. Now I'm well rid of it!"

"Azmachis? Azmachis?"

"Yes, great soothsayer! grand reader of sand fleas! I know now that the mysterious man who gave me the armlet was one of Azmachis' men. Azmachis was marking me, so that no matter where I went his spies would instantly recognize me and could keep me under surveillance."

"Well then, by the same token, the armlet must have saved your life a dozen times over. His men would recognize you by the armlet and know that you were not to be harmed, because you were valuable to Azmachis."

"That is probably true," Thurms conceded. "But I want no favors from the likes of that bloody-minded rogue. Those tribesmen back there are welcome to the accursed object. I'll take care of myself!" *Aton willing,* he added under his breath.

Later he was to reflect that perhaps the armlet *had* been an amulet, and that in throwing it away he had also thrown his luck with it. Because from that time on their luck turned very sour, very sour indeed.

It was in the dead hush of evening when they crackled across the sands and into the last oasis. Thurms and Kipa were busy at the tailgate of the chariot, removing their waterskins and grain sacks and rations and weapons for the night, when a stranger came to call.

Thurms, bending over the platform, his back to Kipa, felt Kipa tap him nervously on the shoulder.

"Thth-thurms."

"Yes? What is it now?"

"Www-we have a vvv-visitor. I thth-think he's come for ddd-dinner."

Not finding Kipa's hesitant stammer at all to his liking, Thurms straightened up and turned around and found himself staring into the cold liquid eyes of a lioness.

She was twenty yards off and she was mouse-colored and old and mangy. But she still had teeth. She hunkered down in the turf that spread among the boles of the palms and regarded the two men with unblinking, conscienceless eyes. The plumed tip of her tail twitched.

With the utmost caution Thurms started to bend at the knees, sinking slowly to bring his right hand in contact with the case of javelins he had placed on the sand beside his feet.

The hide on the lioness' back rippled, and her shoulders rolled slightly forward. Thurms froze indecisively. When she charged, he knew, it would be in two long bounds and a short one, with the tail guiding her like the feathers on an arrow straight to the bull's-eye. He would have to try to catch her with a javelin on the last leap; that would be the high one, when she had to spring upward and when for just one second her tawny chest would be exposed.

The lioness started to move—not charging yet, merely shortening the distance for the charge that was to come.

She crept in a straight line, hunkered down and taking cautiously dainty steps, stop and go, stop and go . . .

All at once the wind was right (or wrong) and the harnessed team picked up her scent and backrolled their starting eyes fearfully and spooked on the spot, bolting out of there as if they'd been fired from a catapult, the empty chariot bouncing and careening behind them, as the startled lioness right-angled her supple body with a look of distraction in her bright hungry eyes and broke into a tan blur of motion right after the fleeing team.

Thurms and Kipa ran through the palm-columned oasis shouting for all they were worth. But it was no good: the team and the chariot were long gone for the north. There was no telling about the lion.

For the first time Thurms was afraid of the desert. Behind them lay the life-giving chain of oases; before them the wasteland of the desert of Sinai. Far far across the seemingly flat expanse of sand stood the vague barrier of the Range. You would think that as long as you could see it you could walk to it, but he knew how deceptive distance could be in a desert—treacherously deceptive.

Kipa, evidently, was harboring the same misgivings—beginning to doubt that the off chance of finding a lost city and a fortune in treasure was worth risking their lives for, and he said as much.

"Perhaps it is a dream after all. Perhaps there is no Tenakertom. Perhaps we are marching ourselves into this heat trap for nothing."

"Perhaps," Thurms murmured.

"Perhaps we should turn back while we still have the opportunity?"

But Thurms didn't want to turn back. He was thinking of Kemheb's words . . . *adventure is man pitting himself against the magnitude and mysteries of nature, seeking the unknown, following the world's lost paths to their hidden conclusions.* And he used Bek as an excuse for going on.

"We still have to find Bek, remember. That's Horemheb's order."

"The scourge of Set on Bek! And the fangs of Asyut in Horemheb—where they'll do the most good! What do we care about Bek? We will probably find his bleached bones twenty miles on, and what will we have proved by it, and who will be the better for it?"

Thurms readjusted the waterskin on his back. They were each lugging one full skin and one full pack of rations. Thurms carried a bow and a quiver of arrows, and Kipa a javelin.

"Well then, think of the treasure," he offered. "Suppose it *does* exist? Suppose it is waiting for us right out there?" He pointed.

Kipa thought of the treasure. "Let us go on," he said instantly.

They went on.

A desert is a distant planet, unpeopled. A desert is an endless ocean without ships. A sea of sand, a white and blue world. It was a land without shadows. No friendly tree, no gaunt rock to throw a spoke of shade on the dehydrated sands. Thurms and Kipa were two puny little specks lurching through an immensity of burning space.

They went forward with the sense of two men on a log in the middle of an ocean.

Ocean—sea. Men always thought of the desert in that relation. Because of the waves of sand. Because of the loneliness and emptiness and nothingness. Because of man's helplessness if anything goes wrong; in this case—water.

On the third day of their stumbling and sand-slogging their food ran out. But that wasn't as important as the water. The army had taught Thurms how to provide for himself in the desert—as long as he had his own water.

He and Kipa set snares at the mouths of little burrows in the sand, the doorways of subterranean homes for the fennecs, a long-eared carnivorous sand-fox no bigger than a small rabbit.

The trouble with setting snares was that it meant they had to spend the night in one place in order to return to their traps at dawn. And desert nights are cold nights. The diurnal death of the sun was a quick silent death, and then the chill of the desert air covered them like an icy blanket. Kipa dug himself a hole in the sand and lay there like a fat hog moaning and chattering and mumbling curses about 'false Aton' and 'false Ammon' and all the other gods who had let him down: not forgetting to place a hearty curse upon Thoth, who seemed quite at home inside Kipa's indescribably filthy garments and who slept the sleep of the wicked, cursed or not.

Their net catch at dawn was one small fennec.

"If we had the time to spare," Thurms said, "we could pick up the tracks of one of them and follow them to the fennecs' pasture-ground. They go where there are small dry shrubs and eat the snails they find on the twigs."

"You mean, if we had the *water* to spare," Kipa corrected. "Come, come, sluggish master. Let us get on. I have a horror of exhausting our water supply while we are still in this sand trap you forced me to explore. The Range still looks as far off as when we started."

It did indeed. And it seemed to stay that way for many days. Always there, always in front of them, always serenely remote and unobtainable.

The bright hard sky glittered like a new-honed knife. The desert had become an anvil and Thurms and Kipa staggered under the hammer-strokes of the sun. They pushed on into the golden emptiness. Thurms threw away his helmet; Kipa threw away the javelin; Thurms threw away the quiver of arrows, then the bow; Kipa thought about throwing away the worthless Thoth, but decided against it in the end. Perhaps there was still a little luck left in the god. Who could tell?

And finally, inevitably, their water ran out.

They were imprisoned in a white circle, captives of the grim tyrant Thirst. Water, the element without taste, color, or odor, that is not necessary to life but is rather life itself, was the only thought left in their burnt-out skulls.

Water water water . . . and before them, on their flanks, and behind them stretched sand sand sand . . .

Lost cities had become childish dreams. Vast treasures held no more importance than a cup of sand. To drink water was the key to existence. Water, crystal clear, cold and gurgling; that's what Thurms thought of. No—that's what he thought during the first long steaming day. After that he thought of any kind of water: scummy, brackish, silty, torpid, anything that would pass as water.

He suddenly realized that all men were tied to the earth by invisible ropes of water. Those ropes were Life and they would let a man go only so far. Thurms and Kipa had now gone one step beyond the boundary and they had broken their connection.

Yet to turn back was physically impossible. Their libidos had been sized by the vertigo of empty space and it would drag them on and on like a human magnet. The two of them—the young soldier who was a general's son, and the rascal who was probably an escaped slave—gasp-lurched along in the relentless drag of the inexorable horizon.

And always waiting ahead of them was the distant, unapproachable backbone of the desert, the Range.

"An oasis! I see a beautiful oasis!" Kipa suddenly cried. "O Maut, save me! I take back the one or two thoughtless and unkindly remarks I might have made in my desperation regarding the characters of Aton and Ammon and all the rest too numerous to mention! See! See! Blind master! See the tall beautiful palms waving, beckoning us on?"

Thurms looked and saw the heat haze rising from the shimmering sands.

"A mirage," he said shortly. "I've seen them before."

"Lies! Lies! I *see it* I tell you! It is right in front of you!"

"Kipa, try not to lose what little sense you have. It is a mirage, I tell you: a trick of the heat reflection and the eye."

Kipa wouldn't listen to the information. He concatenated a dozen or so unpleasant words and fired them all over Thurms.

"You're trying to misguide me! You want me to die out

here! You want the treasure of Tenakertom all for your greedy self!"

Thurms thought about it and decided that it was a good cause to put into effect. "Truly you *are* a soothsayer, Kipa! For behold, you have guessed my plan. Well, farewell, robber of tombs! I'm off to Tenakertom! I'll leave you to your mirage oasis." And he turned and walked on toward the Range.

Kipa cast a last despairing look at his 'oasis,' and started toiling after Thurms. "Wait! Wait! Foul, false Egyptian! You cannot cheat me of my treasure! Wait, you son of a general disorder!"

They saw many mirages that day, so vividly clear that at times even Thurms was ready to believe in them, the most popular being the village built upon an island in the midst of a lake. Yet as they approached, the boundary of the apparent water retreated, drawing further and further back until there was nothing.

Sometimes the concave rays of light showed them marvelous things: great cities and forts, obelisks and spires, basaltic precipices and forests of naked trees, and always lakes . . . water water water.

The force of the Sinai sun made Thurms feel as though he were walking in a warm, deep sea of glue. His lips were parched. He could no more have spat saliva than he could have spat pieces of gold.

He began to talk to himself. Perhaps because Kipa was too far behind to talk to. Or perhaps because he was approaching the first stage of desert madness. Certainly the 'talk' was not rational . . .

Do you think you need water?

"I *know* I need water."

No, only because you think you do. Don't think about it. Then you won't need it.

"Well, what of my fatigue, then? I feel as if I've lost my immortal life, and that my body is already dead and useless."

No. If your body is dead, then you are your immortal life. Then your body can feel no pain, no thirst. Think of it like that.

Thurms thought of it but it did him little good. His body and he were still one, and at every step it screamed its pain, its thirst.

"I've failed. It doesn't work. I cannot go on."

Very well, then. Think of something simple. Think of the treasure. Think of Kemheb and Bek. They are waiting for you at Tenakertom.

Thurms raised his head and looked at the bleary Range and he thought of Tenakertom and for a while he forgot about water. And he went on.

At sunset they came across an old dying one-hump camel. It was down on its right side in the sand, its four long legs with the thick callous cushions shoved straight out as though trying to hold back something expected but as yet unseen, its long sun-shading eyelashes closed, and a death-rattle slobbering through its oblique nostrils.

Thurms put the sorry animal to rest with one merciful blow of his bronze-bladed sword. Kipa shook his head dolefully, saying:

"I'd rather eat uncooked fennecs than camel meat."

"Fat fool—he might have some water left in his sacks."

It was not a pretty job but certainly a necessary one. Thurms cut open the paunch and into the structure of the stomach and removed a number of pouches. Thurms and Kipa had water that night; not much, but much much better than nothing.

The next day they staggered through the sun-scorched remains of a scattered, half-buried antediluvian forest in the sand and made a discovery. A perfectly sound chariot stood idle among the petrified branches and stumps and black marble logs which littered the ground.

The grim remains of a team, still in harness, was in a tangle before the chariot. The bones had been picked clean, of course, but they didn't have that bone-white look of old desert-bleached bones.

"Recent," Kipa commented. Thurms nodded, walking around the abandoned chariot. It was a work vehicle, larger and more cumbersome than the springy little war chariots.

Where did it come from? Where was it going? What became of the driver? How long ago? Thurms looked across the dunes at the Range. It seemed suddenly closer to him; but perhaps only because he wanted it to seem so. He no longer trusted his vision.

"Let us get on."

They pushed on into the heat, their leaden feet dragging in the clinging sand, as though wading toward a fortress through a field of boiling pitch spilled from huge jars.

Thurms raised his head and said, "Look, poppies."

"Very humorous, cruel master," Kipa said disparagingly, head down.

Thurms rubbed his eyes. The poppies were still there, but he said nothing. He waited to see if they would recede the way a proper mirage should when advanced upon. They didn't.

"Kipa. I'm certain that I actually see poppies."

"Why must you torture me so?" Kipa wailed, not bothering to look up. "I've lost my faith in mirages. I don't wish to see any more of them. I can't stand the sight of all that cruel, false water. Please do not bother me again until your mirage goes away."

"But it *isn't* going away. Kipa! *It's standing still!* Kipa, for Set's sake, it isn't a mirage. It's an oasis!"

He started running—across the last stream of sand and into the poppies that stretched away from him like a colorful prayer rug to a far-off barrier of palm trees. He ran into a new world, searching.

10

THE SNAKE PIT

THE LAND WAS crowded with poppies in wide, unbroken fields, right up to the foothills of the mountain wall. They nodded, leaned toward each other, they seemed to whisper, as Thurms and Kipa sloughed through them—heedless of their beauty—with their battered sandals.

And in their center, like a diamond on a board of gold, a clear still pool sparked in the sun.

They went mad in the water, throwing themselves headlong into the pool, intent upon drinking it dry. They drank and sucked and guzzled and submerged themselves and splashed each other and laughed like a contented pair of crazy men, and drank some more and kept it up until they became sick and had to crawl out on hands and knees and retch. Then they returned to drink again.

Thoth scrambled out of Kipa's soggy clothes in a hysteria of haste, giving Kipa one good whack after another with his tail in the process. He wasn't in favor of the bath at all. Kipa picked up his pet and dried him carefully with poppy petals, then scouted up all manner of little crawly tasty things to appease Thoth's temper, stating to Thurms:

"Didn't I tell you he would bring us luck? He has led us to the Range exactly as he showed us he would on the sand map in Tanis! O Thoth! You remarkable eight-footed god!"

Thurms grinned at his friend. "Out in the desert you didn't seem so sure of Thoth. You seemed more inclined toward Ammon and Aton then."

Kipa snapped his fingers contemptuously.

"A sow's ear for Ammon and Aton! They have no more idea of what they are doing than two silly old women looking for diamonds along the banks of the Nile! Thoth can dance rings around them!"

"Even so, a little more consistency would be a welcome chan—"

"Shush! Shush!" Kipa cried, covering Thoth with his palms to shelter his delicate little ears from Thurms' rude voice. "Do you want him to hear you? Do you want to hurt his feelings with all this nonsense of Ammon and Aton? The first thing you know he will take away our good luck. Then where shall we be?"

Thurms was wondering where they were right then. He stood up and stared across the poppies and sand streams to the looming wall of the Range.

. . . somewhere out there, lost among the trackless dunes, there is an old old well—Seken's Well—and from its rim may be seen Anar's Arch. And that is the key. He listened to his memory, to the words Kemheb had planted there.

"Kipa, we have water here and an oasis over there for shade and dates, but we still haven't found the Key to Tenakertom."

Instantly Kipa was all business. He picked up Thoth and led the way to a sand patch. "We will leave the matter entirely in Thoth's capable hands—er feet," he announced in a manner that implied great personal conceit—being the sole owner of the indefatigable Thoth.

A map was traced in the sand: the Range to the southeast, the desert to the north, a poppy stuck in the center to represent the oasis they had discovered. Thoth was gently placed beside the poppy.

"Now," Kipa said eagerly, "whichever direction he chooses to follow along the foot of the Range, east or west, will be the direction in which we will find Seken's Well!"

This time there was no hesitation or backwardness about Thoth. He started headlong for the east . . . where there was an ant, which he quickly caught and ate.

"It's an omen!" Kipa cried.

"It's an ant," Thurms disagreed.

"Of course it's an ant," Kipa said testily. "I know it's an ant. But it represents Seken's Well. It's an omen, witless idiot!"

"It doesn't represent a well. It represents a meal, stupid cow!"

"Very well. V-e-r-y well! We will do it again."

He set Thoth back by the poppy and Thoth quickly got underway and returned right to the spot where he had previously found the ant.

"An omen! Any fool can see it's an omen—just as if Osiris had reached down and slapped your empty head!"

"It's not a fair test," Thurms maintained. "He returned to the same place to see if he could find another ant."

Kipa romped around in the weeds in a rage of frustration and threw handfuls of sand in his face and asked Ammon and Aton and one or two others to behold what the desert sun had done to Thurms' mind.

Thurms, who had his own atavistic share of superstition, was half inclined to believe that Kipa was right. An omen was an omen. Still—that business of the ant bothered him.

Finally he gave Kipa a kick in the part of him that presented the most target, and told him that the best plan would be a compromise.

"We shall separate. You'll go east and I'll look west. We'll each go as far as we can until dark, then we'll double back and meet at the oasis."

So it was arranged. They filled their waterskins, stuffed themselves with dates, wished each other good luck, and set out in opposite directions.

Thurms stayed with the sand rises and gentle-rolling hillocks which meandered brokenly through the poppies, looking down on the glittering, undulating fields, searching for —for what? The term 'well' was ambiguous in the desert. It might mean a simple hand-dug hole in the earth, or it might mean a true, circular, stone-lined shaft, or it might simply mean a natural spring.

His biggest concern was that the poppies might have grown over the well's opening, or that it had been filled in by countless sandstorms. He kept glancing at the distant Range, thinking that perhaps they should just forget the well entirely and concentrate on finding Anar's Arch— whatever that was.

And that in itself would be no simple chore. The Range was like an old fortress wall that had been breached many times and fallen into a woeful state of neglect. Countless gorges and canyons showed themselves to his view, and the Arch might be in any of them. All of which led him to one conclusion: the reason for the Key was that Seken's Well must be laid on a direct line with a canyon known as Anar's Arch. And without the well as a starting point a man could easily spend the rest of his life prowling through the multitude of blind gorges, until he was lost, worn out and mad.

Something in the nature of a track caught his eyes in the poppies below. He hurried down a gorsy slope and into the weeds and flowers. The poppies had been mashed and trampled into a narrow pathway as though from a team and chariot. And the track was recent, very recent.

Bek, he said.

He started walking, following what he was certain was Bek's weedy wake. The tracks, he noticed after a while, followed a sort of mad pattern. They would cut across a level patch of poppies to a sand rise, follow the base of the hillock for a way, then turn obliquely into the open again and run off to another rise. The reason for this unorthodox zigzag course was apparent: Bek in his chariot had been doing what Thurms had done on his feet—going from rise to rise, leaving his chariot to run up to the summits to survey the flatlands below, hoping to spot Seken's Well from an elevated position.

Thurms stayed with the path, following it doggedly hour after hour. He didn't know what else to do.

The sun was preparing to take its last giant step down for the day when Thurms scrambled to the top of a rise for a final look. After that he would have to start back for the oasis. He stood on the quiet, sand-blowing hill and cast his eyes over the darkening poppy fields below. Just as he started to turn away he spotted the suggestion of a cuplike depression in the flowers.

He couldn't make out what it was. The distance was too great and the waning light was tricky. The poppies nodded and trembled and rippled in the sunset breeze. Sometimes he lost sight of the circular indentation completely. He followed the chariot tracks with his eyes. Dimly he could see where they had gone in the direction of the little depression, but from his position they seemed to have passed it by about sixty feet. After that the tracks were lost to him.

He hurried down the slope and started into the grass-blowing field, cutting obliquely away from the chariot track.

Now that he had lost his elevation the cuplike depression was no longer visible. Fearing that the oncoming twilight would catch him short, he started to run. He glanced up at the Range to get his bearings. The mountain barrier stood directly in front of him and he caught a glimpse of the opening of a dark gorge. And something else—for just a brief moment—a far, small stone crown arched against the milky-blue sky.

Anar's Ar . . .

The grass under his right foot flung forward and his body lurched into a sickening tilt as his left foot came down on nothing, nothing at all. His equilibrium wrenched away from his fast-moving body and with a cry of alarm snagged in his throat he toppled into a dizzy somersault into blackness.

He didn't think he had been knocked unconscious, merely stunned into a mental suspension for a few moments. Slowly, he gathered his outraged wits together and started to move his pain-grabbing body.

There were blunt, hard objects under him and he rolled away from them and found soft cool sand with his hands. He looked up and around with a peering, startled intensity. The light was like the light in an undersea cave, and it was getting worse. With a sense of incredulous awe he realized the truth.

I was looking for Seken's Well and I fell into it!

He almost gave a shout of joy. He had not only found the well, he had even caught a glimpse of Anar's Arch! But he restrained his jubilation, remembering where he was. He would have to extricate himself first and celebrate later. He could hardly wait to see Kipa's fat expression of gawking amazement. Him and his ant-eating god!

He shoved up to his feet painfully and stood on shaky legs, looking.

It was a well that nature had made, not man, and it had dried up long long ago. The only water it contained now was that which was trickling from the split waterskin at his feet. It must have helped to break his fall. The thirsty sand sponged the last of the liquid.

It was a tear-shaped pit, fat and round at the bottom, narrow at the top, like a ballas water jar. The diameter of the sand floor was about twenty feet. It was cluttered with rocks, shale, and old bones and feathers. The presence of the feathers rather puzzled him. There was a large cone-shaped mound of sand in the exact center of the well. He understood that. It was the accumulation of drifted sand that had rained through the circular opening above.

It was that opening that bothered him. It was only six feet wide and it was twelve feet above the floor of the well.

To think of trying to climb up there was absurd: no man could scale those concave walls. In the last of the filtered daylight he explored the pit. There was a shalelike composition for a foundation, then graduating layers of crumbly dirt, and finally the upper out-of-reach layer of hard-packed sand. There were numerous small cracks and fissures in the aged earthen walls, and if the sides of the pit were only vertical he might be able to use them for hand- and footholds. As it was they were useless. He couldn't climb upside down.

He picked his way through the rocks and shale, disconsolately. The pit had a musty malodorous scent, but he might as well get used to it, because he knew now that he was going to have to spend the night there. Kipa would make no attempt to find him until morning. Even then it might take Kipa most of the day before he finally located the mouth of the well. But—suppose he *didn't* find it?

Thurms looked up at the circular opening. It was a round

glow of dark blue. The pit was now black. A crawling sense of apprehensive dread came over him. He shuddered.

All at once he started to shout.

Stop it! Get hold of yourself, for Set's sake. Save your voice for tomorrow. Kipa is miles from you now.

He wondered just how far his voice would carry from this subterranean tomb. Then his throat felt dry and he cursed the trick the gods had played on him by having him burst his waterbag. But, with a stab of contrition, he took it back. Cursing gods wasn't a safe practice—especially for a man in his position. He cursed Thoth instead. If it hadn't been for his voracious ant hunger Thurms and Kipa would still be together; at least Thurms would be there in the pit and Kipa would be up above devising the means to get him out.

Yet exactly how would Kipa go about getting him out? No ladder, no ropes, nothing to serve as a rope. A cold damp sweat broke over Thurms' body. The more he reviewed his situation the worse it became. He began to pace in the lonely darkness, thinking.

His first idea was to start digging an inclined tunnel, a sloping passageway through which he could crawl upwards. But there were drawbacks to that: he might run into buried boulders which would prove to be impassable, or the upgrading tunnel might suffer a disastrous cave-in when it reached the layers of sand.

He discarded the tunnel idea and switched to another method. It was the cone-shaped heap of sand in the center of the floor that gave him the inspiration. He would build it up, add to the heap until it was high enough for him to stand on and to reach and grab Kipa's hand—if Kipa found him.

He shook his head impatiently. There was no sense in thinking about Kipa not finding him: that would lead to madness. He set himself the task of thinking positively.

Kipa *would* find him. He would find him tomorrow. And Thurms would be ready for him.

The moon was up now and a ghostly glow diffused the floor of the pit, leaving the concave walls in a shroud of utter black, giving the centralized sand pile the luminous aspect of a rearing night monster. Thurms set to work at once.

First he gathered up all the sizable rocks he could see or find with his groping hands, and he used them to shore up the foundation of the sand heap. It took a long time and a great deal of doing, because he knew that he would need a broad, sturdy base upon which to build his cairn. He worked until he was exhausted, until his head was nodding on his neck and he found himself losing his balance repeatedly. So he gave up for a while, just long enough to catch a catnap . . . he thought.

It was an insidious noise that awoke him. He opened his eyes to darkness, but not to the black of night. He glanced up. The circular opening above his head showed the rosy sheen of dawn. He started to get up, but stalled. He had heard the noise again; a soft, barely-audible rustling; a dry dirt-sliding sound, coming closer and closer and . . .

A short dark snake dropped from nowhere and twisted itself into a coil on the shale-strewn floor. Thurms reached for his sword.

Something cold and muscular and moving dropped *thhlop* on his bare back and he sprang straight up with a cry as another snake slipped from his shoulder to the sand and went away into the heavy shadows in zigzag alarm.

He looked wildly around, his skin starting to prickle. The rustling sound was coming, coming, multiplying in volume, and a small round head emerged from the dirt wall by his left shoulder and two very small beady eyes stared at him.

Then the head dropped and a tubular body slid down down down and plopped at his feet.

He sprang sideways, raising the bronze-bladed sword. Out of the walls—out of the numerous little cracks and fissures—dozens of dark-gleaming serpents were sliding, dropping limply to the floor.

Spellbound with horror and revulsion he watched them coming, sliding and dropping, writhing and coiling, hissing at him. The old dried-up well was a snake pit for nocturnal reptiles that prowled through the weeds and poppies and sand searching for prey in the light of the moon. Evidently they aestivated here in the cool shadow of the pit during the prolonged heat of the day. And they didn't seem to be in favor of his intrusion.

He had a nodding acquaintance with many of the desert reptiles, and he thought he recognized this particular variety—though it was hard to be certain in the dim pit light of dawn. They were nonvenomous, and—taken one at a time—harmless to man. But Thurms' predicament was akin to a beetle finding itself in a jar filled with worms. He rather thought that by sheer numbers alone they could do him in.

He started backing away from them, taking care where he stepped. The uneven floor was acrawl with the ghastly things. They were all around the sides of the pit in coiling clumps. He couldn't tell how many there were. The undulating movements in the heavy shadows gave the impression of hundreds.

He backed up onto his bulwarked sand mound and found that he was sharing it with one of the reptiles. The thing reared its head, opened its jaws and hissed. He chopped with his sword, then flipped the two thrashing halves into the shadows with the point of his blade.

"Kipa!" He raised his face to the round mouth of the well above him and yelled with all his might. *"KIPA!"*

Sssssssss—sss—ssssss

He looked down. Spearheads of the main snake mass were wiggling toward him, coming at the mound on all sides like wheel spokes to a hub. He stepped to the edge on his right and started hacking, then back and to the left and cleared them away from that vicinity, then across the mound to a sector where four of them were actually snaking over the edge of the rock embankment, and then hurried back to the original point of attack, one of them taking a pass at his left ankle as he stopped, and he swung the blade left, then right, then right again. It was a brisk minute.

He cleared his stronghold and stood swaying and sweating and gasping from exertion. The pit suddenly seemed airless. He looked up at the bright circle of freedom and fresh air right over his head. So near—yet so Set-cursed far!

The entire mass body of the serpents was greatly agitated now. They coiled and writhed and squirmed among themselves, and dark clumps of them started slithering toward the mound, their slick bodies rustling dryly across the sand. He fought them, hacking and chopping and flinging them off, their hisses compressing his tortured eardrums. He fought them with loathing and hate and an atavistic repugnance that was bringing him to the point of screaming savagery.

They kept coming, quicker now than he could blade them off. He kicked at them with his feet, sending the twisting, hissing S-shaped bodies flying. He grabbed up his torn waterskin in his left hand and beat them back. Sometimes the bronze blade of his sword would become useless to him as one or two alive or dying serpents would entangle themselves about it and ride there until he had to snatch them off with his hand.

He felt the cold, hard-muscle bodies slithering over his feet. He felt them entwining around his ankles, felt the sharp, piercing burn of their back-fanged bites. He kicked and hacked and beat. He fought himself into a fury of insanity. And then—exhausted, half-blind, sick with vertigo—he dropped where he stood and sprawled among the still-writhing corpses of his enemies.

The snakes had retreated. He wondered for how long. He wondered if he had the voice left to call to Kipa for help. He listened to the subdued hissing and dry sand-rustling and slithering in the shadows. He shuddered with a loathing that went beyond horror. It was a sickness of the soul. What he had been through was more than the mental balance of man was equipped to face.

I'll go mad if I don't get out of here soon, he thought. And then he passed out.

When he came to he realized that he had won . . . at least the first round. There were hardly any snakes left in the pit. The bulk of them had already taken themselves off through their little subterranean tunnels. The few that were left he killed or harassed until they fled.

He stood at one side of the sand mound, leaning on his stained sword, and marshaled his thoughts.

This was the serpents' home and he had every reason to expect that they would return—if not today, then surely in the morning. As far as he knew a snake had no mind, therefore no memory—so they would be ready to take him on again as soon as they returned. And this time he knew he would lose. He would go stark mad. He was quite certain of that.

He went to work industriously on his sand, rock and shale cairn, pausing every so often to send a shout up for that Set-cursed Kipa, whom he bitterly pictured as loafing about the oasis catching fennecs and stuffing himself with dates and water. The original sand mound was nearly as sturdy as a stalagmite, having calcified during the ages, and on this base he added a layer of rock and shale, stopping only when he had exhausted his supply. Then he went to work on the walls of the pit, using the point of his sword to gouge out more rocks and huge carbon-hardened dirt clods.

He worked without cessation, toiling against time—against night, against dawn, against the return of the serpents.

All at once he stopped in the act of heaving a stone onto his cairn, his head cocked to one side like an animal listening.

Thhhhur-mmms . . .

It was a far-away prolonged cry, like a lost voice wailing in a wilderness. Thurms leaped to the top of his mound and tilted his face to the mouth of the well.

"KIPA! HERE! KII-*PA!*"

He listened, distracted by the echoing ring of his own voice in the pit. Then—*Thhhur-mmms*—again. And closer. Much closer this time. He bellowed Kipa's name as it had never been bellowed before. And he kept it up until his voice cracked and strangled and faded to a mere whisper. But it didn't matter: good old lovable, Aton-blessed Kipa had found the well.

"Is it truly my master I see below me?" Kipa cried rapturously, his moony face and bald head appearing at the mouth of the well. "You shouldn't treat your devoted servant in this shoddy manner. You shouldn't leave him to spend the night in this Maut-cursed wilderness by himself. Don't you realize that a pack of jackals came to the oasis to pester me? I had to spend the night in a palm tree, and I slept most uncomfortably, let me tell you. What kind of a fix have you stupidly gotten yourself into?"

"A snake pit. Hurry and get me out."

"A snake pit? Couldn't you find a less disagreeable place

to sleep in?" He sprawled himself on his fat belly at the lip of the well and reached down as Thurms reached up. A blank space of nearly thirty inches intervened between their straining fingers.

"Kipa, listen to me. Remove that mummy shroud you refer to as your robe and lower it down to me. Be sure you have a firm grasp on your end. Wrap it about one of your wrists."

Kipa agreed that he would do so—with the firm understanding that if he felt himself slipping, Thurms would instantly let go and not pull his 'devoted servant' into the snake pit.

"Kipa, when I get out of here I am going to thrash you soundly with a stick!" Thurms vowed. "Now lower your robe or I'll toss some snakes up for you to play with!"

"Wait until I find a safe place for Thoth. I don't want him to wander off and get lost, you know. My robe is the only home he knows."

"Give him some ants to eat and he'll be happy," Thurms said caustically.

Just as he started to kick at the air and haul himself hand over hand, Kipa let out a cry and nearly let go of the twisted robe.

"Anar's Arch! I see Anar's Arch!"

Thurms, his stomach in the back of his throat from the sharp drop he had just taken, cursed through gritted teeth.

"Of course, you fat fool! This is Seken's Well."

Kipa had already grasped that fact for himself, and when he spoke again his voice sounded hoarse and urgent.

"Hurry, Thurms, hurry! I see something more than Anar's Arch."

"What?" Thurms gasped, struggling up the twisting, turning robe.

"Smoke. Someone is making a fire in that gorge."

11

ANAR'S ARCH

THE GORGE RAN straight and true back to a formidable wall of stone as if the arm of a god had thrust open the passage. It was strewn with great boulders, leaving only a narrow shale gangway through the center. It was a lonely, brooding place—in a sense, ghostly, and Thurms and Kipa glanced at each other occasionally without speaking a word, their eyes reaching out like trembling hands to assure themselves that they were together. Thurms couldn't help thinking it would make an ideal site for Tut's tomb: at least in Tut's morbid eye.

They could see the smoke quite clearly now, drifting up before the face of the wall of stone, right up to the looming stone arch at the top two hundred feet above. They couldn't see the fire yet, or the person who had made it.

Abruptly they did. A bareheaded man in the wing-end corselet and short tunic of a soldier stepped from behind a boulder and confronted them with a bow and arrow in his hands. For a brief moment he seemed as startled by their appearance as they were by his, but he recovered quickly and raised an arm in salutation.

Thurms had expected to find Bek, or even Kemheb, but the man standing before him was the last man on earth he was prepared to see.

"Hail, Thurms! Come join the merry little band of deserters!"

Hritut grinned his crocodile grin.

Bek was sitting before a fire in a cup-shaped hollow at the base of the stone wall. His chariot was parked off to one side and the hobbled team was nonchalantly muzzling karoo shrubs and cropping a patch of gama grass—the same chariot and team that had once fetched Thurms and Bek to Fort Harba.

The seasoned commander looked up at Thurms without a hint of expression on his tough soldier's face, and grunted.

"So, Thurms, you had to try for Tenakertom after all." He pulled at his broken nose and gave a mirthless snort. "What a prize catch we'd make for Horemheb. A commander, a general's son, and a wastrel from one of Thebes' most influential families!"

Thurms glanced at the bewildered-looking Kipa and gave a quick, almost imperceptible shake of his head. Bek and Hritut thought he too was a deserter. He would just as soon leave it at that for the moment. Now he not only had the surly, capable Bek to deal with but the insidious Hritut as well. They had both deserted the army for the sake of a lost treasure and he didn't think that they would be willing to conduct themselves as reasonable men.

He adopted a negative attitude, hunkering down across the fire from Bek and bringing some dates from his pouch. He popped them into his mouth and talked around them.

"I expected to find you rolling in wealth by now, Bek.

Why are you wasting your time in this gorge? Haven't you found Tenakertom yet?"

Hritut gave a sour laugh and Bek glowered at the fire.

"Your so-called Key to Tenakertom isn't worth a Set's curse," Bek said angrily. "We've been sitting in this stinking rock trap for three days!"

Thurms couldn't understand. "But why? You found Seken's Well, didn't you? And you've certainly found Anar's Arch."

"But we haven't been able to *reach* Anar's Arch!" Bek made a violent gesture with his hand at the rising dark face of stone looming over them. "Four times I've tried to scale that. Every time I've been stopped by that outcropping of rock you see above you. The last time I tried I slipped from the face when I was ten yards up and sprained my ankle." He turned a look of pure hate on Hritut.

"And this marsh rat of Thebes doesn't have the guts of a man to try it. Not even once!"

Hritut wet his lips and smirked. His eyes shifted in his face and he glanced nervously upward at the great frowning wall of stone.

"Do you think I'm a fool?" he asked. "I don't want to die like a dropped egg. Besides—" he fished in his pouch and brought out a polished stone scarab, held it in his hand for them to see, "I've been making sacrifice to my scarab god. I've been pleading with him to show us a way to surmount this obstacle: and lo—now we have Thurms! Surely a mere stone wall will not deter a general's son from obtaining his objective!" He grinned at Thurms.

Thurms stood up to contemplate the stone barrier. It was as vertical as the wall of a fort, and nearly as smooth. Undoubtedly it had been the backboard of a waterfall in some dim age. Certainly it was old, for the face was lined and cracked with a multitude of small fissures. There were foot-

and handholds to spare for a climber, and the wall at its steepest leaned back from the straight, lending a climber a distinct advantage against the gravitation pull. But right above that point the trouble began.

It was a bump of craggy old rock, like a bare brow overhanging a sunken, noseless face. It was a gigantic blister, fifty-sixty feet in diameter. To reach the outermost point of safety (the apex of the bump) would be like setting a scaling ladder against a wall and trying to climb up the underside of the rungs.

Thurms sat down again and rubbed at his mouth, speculating. Bek watched him darkly; Hritut grinned at him. Kipa sat off by himself in the shale and sand and remained unobtrusively mute. The presence of the two desperate Egyptian deserters made him apprehensive. He didn't have to read the sands to know that trouble was hovering over all of them like the heavy hand of Set.

"Very well," Thurms said shortly. "I'll make an attempt in the morning." Then he asked them about Kemheb: hadn't they seen any trace of him?

Bek shrugged and stared broodingly at the fire. He didn't care a fig about Kemheb or anyone else. His mind was on reaching Tenakertom. Kemheb's welfare held no interest for Hritut either. He said:

"Who cares about him? We don't need him now. I've had my own problems since I saw you last. You'll never know what I've been through to reach this place." Then he proceeded to oppose the stated fact that Thurms would 'never know' by telling him, in detail . . .

Hritut knew the Syrian tongue, so he had understood what Kemheb and Azmachis had said to each other that day in the far-away oasis in the Wilderness of Shur. Azmachis had feared that Kemheb would go off with the two patrol soldiers and share with them his secret to the lost city. He had implored Kemheb to tell him where Tenakertom was located in the Gebal Yelleq Range. Then Thurms had interrupted the heated conversation. But Hritut had heard enough to know that at least there was such a place as Tenakertom, that it wasn't just an old wives' tale as most people believed.

That night, certain that Thurms would never get them out of Azmachis' Khabiri trap alive, Hritut had gambled upon escaping alone and on foot into the hills. Days later, more dead than alive from his wound and exhaustion, he had stumbled into the Plain of Tina. A sheepherder and his family had taken the dazed deserter in and nursed him back to health. By way of thanks for this altruistic action Hritut, upon recovery, had stolen their work chariot and team.

Knowing no more than what he had overheard—that Tenakertom was somewhere in the Gebal Yelleq Range—he had set out to cross the desert of Sinai.

The gods had been against him. He had forced his team beyond the point of endurance and they had died on him. He had crossed the last thirty miles of desert on foot. He had made it to the oasis, but from that point he had no information to go on. So he had started to explore the numerous and deviously twisting gorges of the range, stumbling in and out of one blind alley after another, always returning to the oasis for substance. And that was where Bek had accidentally found him.

They had formed a sort of on-guard partnership and, with the Key Thurms had unwittingly given Bek, they had found Seken's Well and then this gorge below Anar's Arch.

"Well," Hritut said, tag-lining the tale of his adventures, "now that you're here, I suppose there's enough for three of us." He shot a contemptuous look at the silent Kipa. "Or even four, if you must drag your fat friend along."

Bek gave a sudden grunt, coming out of his brood. "Enough—yes. *If* we can reach it."

Thurms looked up at the looming, twilight-darkling stone face. The bump of brow frowned down upon him forbiddingly. *If,* he thought.

But in the morning he was ready to attempt it, eager even. Because it has always been this way with many many men: confront them with a hill, a cliff, a mountain, and some atavistic compulsion compels them to climb it. First, simply to prove to themselves and to no one else in the world (because no one else matters when it comes to a mountain) that they *can* climb it; second, simply to see what is on the other side. Adventure is man pitting himself against the magnitude and mysteries of nature . . .

Bek, that farsighted veteran, had had the sense to fetch along some scaling ropes from Harba, and he and Hritut now knotted them securely together and into a tight coil that Thurms could loop over his shoulder. While they were thus engaged Kipa had a quiet word with Thurms.

"Master, master, be exceedingly careful when you attempt this ascent. If anything were to happen to you, if you were to slip and fall, *I'd* be left alone in the company of those two desperate villains! I know they'd do me in! I can read it in their crafty eyes!"

Thurms had to grin at Kipa's solicitousness. "Now, Kipa, try to conduct yourself like a hearty adventurer, which I know you are, and not like a craven coward. Do you want me to attempt the climb or not?"

"W-e-l-l . . ."

"Think of the treasure, Kipa."

Kipa thought of the treasure. He broke into a sweat and licked his lips and blinked his porcine eyes rapidly. "Let me give you Thoth to carry, to insure your safe ascent," he offered eagerly.

Thurms thanked him kindly but said *no* thanks. He had no desire to have Thoth crawling all over him as he tried to scale the stone face.

"Ready, Thurms," Bek called, and Thurms walked over to take the rope. But he stopped short. All four of them froze in positions of listening attention. The team cocked their ears and swung their heads down and backwards, looking.

The clack of hoofs and metal felloes came up the gorge. Bek reached for his sword, Hritut for his bow. Kipa looked for somewhere to hide, and Thurms folded his arms over his winged corselet and waited.

A fagged but well-set-up team drew a dusty Egyptian chariot through the rock-ribbed gangway and into the hollow. A lone, fat, bearded man in a robe stood on the platform beaming over with good-fellowship. He drew the team in and raised an arm in salute.

"Hail, mighty warriors of Kem!"

Azmachis removed himself and a plump waterskin from the chariot and gave himself and his team a drink. Stoppering the waterskin with a hemisphere, a hardened cone made of river mud, he replaced it in the chariot and started toward the four stunned men. As far as they could see the only weapon he carried was a harmless ivory-handled fly whisk.

"Ah, Thurms, Thurms!" the fat one cooed. "If I could only find the words to express the joy in my heart over seeing you once again! And my old friend Hritut, too! Truly Ammon is benevolent!" He paused and cocked a knowing eye at the scowling Bek.

"And this would be that worthy commander of Daphnae and later Harba. *Hukukuk!*" he made a soft, fat chuckling noise in his throat. "You see, my spies keep me well informed at all times!" Then he turned to Kipa and gave him a sly poke in his expansive stomach.

"And I've seen this rogue before too, haven't I? Are you still in the market for scorpions, my plump partridge? Eh? Eh?"

Bek was the first one to speak for the Egyptians.

"I take it you're the Khabiri bandit Azmachis. You must be mad to walk in here and deliver yourself into our hands."

Azmachis remained unperturbed by the threat. He smiled greasily at the three soldiers. "Oh no," he said slyly, "I doubt if I have much to fear from three deserters."

Hritut glanced uneasily at Bek and Thurms. They had nothing to say, so the ex-charioteer attempted to bluster.

"And what is to stop us from killing you here and now, out of hand?"

Azmachis made his fat chuckling noise again.

"Thurms is. You see, I know him well. He's a general's son. He will kill willingly in combat or for self-preservation; but it is against his creed to stoop to murder. Eh, Thurms?"

Thurms ignored Azmachis' sophistry. "How did you get here?" he asked bluntly.

"By the simple expedient of following your tracks. Who else would have been heading for the Range? But I seem to have mistimed my arrival. I thought that by now you would have reached Tenakertom and have discovered the treasure."

"The only thing that is keeping us from it is that Set-cursed wall of rock," Hritut growled. "Thurms was just preparing to attempt the ascent for us."

Azmachis looked up at Anar's Arch and expressed his admiration by slapping his rosy cheeks. "Truly a valorous undertaking! One worthy of the General's brave son! Well, well, shall we get on with it?"

"Not so hasty," Bek snarled. "We haven't yet agreed that

you have a share in this venture." He hefted his sword suggestively.

Azmachis was still unruffled. "My lords, let us face the issue squarely: you *must* include me. You have no alternative. I am here and I intend to remain here until I receive my share from the treasure coffers of Tenakertom. If you two soldiers attempt to—uh dispose of me, Thurms will be code-bound to intervene on my behalf. And this rather gross slave of his will, I imagine, join him. You will become a divided camp. Would that be wise? Eh, Commander?"

Bek and Hritut looked at each other indecisively, then at Thurms, who shrugged and said, "There will be enough for five. Let us worry about reaching Tenakertom, instead of cutting each other's throats."

The recent and rapid series of events had set him in a state of bewildered suspension: that is, he couldn't seem to think ahead but could only concentrate on one step at a time. Without doubt the gods, the unseen powers, worked in mysterious ways. They arranged seemingly meaningless meetings, drove people along paths they didn't consciously mean to go. He wondered what the outcome would be, wondered if it were already written in the sands.

Here we are at last, he thought bemusedly. *All of the adventurers finally together—except Kemheb. As though it were ordained from the moment Hritut and I saw that trace of smoke in the sky at Azira's Well. And a fine collection we are . . .*

Bek, with his bred-in-the-bone leader complex. A hardheaded soldier of fortune who profaned everything within sight and many things that were not. Hritut, the craven deserter who believed in a personal god and yet had no faith in his fellow man; and it was impossible to make him see the inconsistency in his theory. And Kipa, the prince of rascals, the escaped slave with a gold bug loose in his sly little brain. And Azmachis, the king of villains, the wiliest, shrewdest cutthroat the Khabiri hordes could offer. And Thurms?

Thurms . . . the young soldier who had finally come to believe that somewhere in this vast crucible of life called Earth, mysteries lay as close-packed as grains of sand on a desert of dunes; that unseen marvels wait around an obscure corner, mute and forgotten; that Tenakertom, the lost city—rife with ancient gold—was waiting, crying out to them, asking why they were blind and deaf to its wonders.

And then he knew that he had always wanted to believe in Tenakertom.

Everything you've ever dreamed of exists . . .

"Hand me the rope," he said to Bek.

It was comparatively easy at first. It was a matter of finding the right handhold and left foothold, then left and higher handhold, then right and higher foothold, and then up and groping, finger-searching with the right hand again. He went up the flat face with arms and legs extended like a spider scrabbling up a wall.

The hollow in the gorge dropped lower and lower beneath him, slowly. The figures of the four men and the features of their anxiously expectant, up-tilted faces shrank in dimension. Then he had to stop looking down. The void that separated him from the ground had grown too great; it created an unhealthy swirl of vertigo. He looked up.

The sun was behind his back. He could feel it burning bright on his skin. Straight up the vivid blue sky stretched like a placid body of water, until it was cut off sharp by the overhang of the brow. He paused and estimated that he had another fifteen feet to go before he would reach the bottom of the overhang. He started up again.

He realized his progress was lagging. He was beginning to feel the down-drag more and more. His arms were starting to ache. Worse—now that he was approaching the beginning of the bump there seemed to be less and less fissures in the old stony face. One thing though, the composition of the rock was changing. It was just rotten enough that, when necessary, he could dig out his own fissures for his hands and feet.

He had left his sword below, taking Bek's dagger which he had stuck in his belt. Now he found a use for it. Hanging by one hand and sometimes on two feet, he scraped and gouged at the crumbly rock with the dagger, making little stepping slots for his toes and fingers.

The gentle swell of the bulge was starting now. He rested again, fighting for his air, sweat running from him as though he were a glob of fat on an inclined oven melting away to nothing. He took one quick glance down. The hollow was a pit, a sun-pooled shaft, the four men and the two horses were antlike. He snatched his eyes away.

He found the first handhold in the underside of the bump and raised his dragging body. Instantly the law of gravitation pulled at his waist. He reached with his left hand, missed, and—like a gate thrown abruptly open, right hand and foot hinging—his body pivoted outward and swung over eternity as the far far hungry earth yawned for him and, wildly, he dug with his left foot, scuffling it across the corroded rock, found something, tested it, brought his left hand back in, got a grip and took a shaky stand.

The sun burned like Set's skillet. The sweat dribbled from his brows into his eyes. He blinked furiously. His arms were leaden with pain and his fingers were bleeding from a crisscross of little rock cuts and his legs were starting to tremble spastically from the strain. All the vast weight of the earth's centripetal pull was hanging from his body.

He reached up with his right hand and his moist nerveless

fingers fumbled over the rough surface of the bump and he found nothing, so he returned that hand to its slot and took a grip and tried with the other, groping and finger-walking, and found something, a sort of little rift, but not enough, and had to bring his left back down and get out the dagger again to try to gouge out a slot in the rift that would give him a safe sure grip.

He moved up, his entire body trembling violently, slick with sweat, half blind, gasping raspingly for air, and raised his head. He thought he understood how he was situated: the outermost point of the bulge was perhaps five feet above his head; there were ready-made cracks and fissures set for him; beyond the center of the bulge the slope would commence to recede, the gravitation tug would cease and he would find himself crouching under the solid security of Anar's Arch.

And it was right at that moment that he knew he wasn't going to make those last five feet.

His arms and legs and fingers and toes simply couldn't do it.

He had forced and strained his extremities too far.

The drag was too much for him. It was the breaking point.

An incredulous horror crept over him. He. Thurms. The General's son was going to die.

"Aton," he gasped, "save me. God . . . help me."

Suddenly he realized it was up to him, to his indomitable spirit, whether he lived or died. It no longer had anything to do with his numb extremities. If he let go then the stone face, the bulge, had beaten him, and his only satisfaction would be the long harrowing drop into the dread eternity waiting, gawking below.

He sucked his breath and bared his teeth like a trapped animal preparing to bite. He inched his left hand up until it joined in the same slot with the right and at the same time his right foot slipped from its tense position and gravity swung him away from the overhung bump and his entire body was attached to the wall by only the eight fingers of his two hands.

He wouldn't relax the frozen, clinging fingers. He hung on, kicking in with his right foot, toe-scratching for a grip that would swing his body inward again. Once he thought he had it but the drag was too heavy and his foot scraped clear.

He tried with the left and felt his toes snub on something. Tried again. Caught. He stalled, sucked air, afraid to move any part or muscle of his strained pain-tightened body.

He had to make the decisive move—which would either be the beginning of the fast-falling end or the continuation of earthly endeavor.

On his left leg he shoved up and reached up and over the apex of the bulge with his right hand and started clawing blindly at anything, everything, for a grip, and found a hold, his fingers biting in like savage teeth, and took most of the weight with that hand as the other went up after it and around it and found a fissure of its own, and then with a biceps-grabbing tug and a lunge and a kick he heaved his stomach onto the center of the bulge and he clung there like a drowsy crab, bathed in sweat, in the hot hard bright strength of the sky.

Anar's Arch loomed overhead. He started climbing for it, hand over foot.

The arch was a natural phenomenon in stone. Probably in some dim period a waterfall had hollowed out the curious formation as it passed under the basaltic rib. A concavo-concave rock gorge drew away from the arch on a gentle upgrade. Thurms dropped the rope and started up the draw.

He reached the issue within fifty yards. Stepping with the care of a superstitious man in a midnight graveyard, he stepped out into an abrupt blaze of noon sun.

Before him lay a wide green bowl, deep in the hands of the clustered hills; circular, small, as though the thumb of a god had run around its edge, shaping it with careful precision.

Halfway up the valley the ruins of Tenakertom began.

12

"EVERYTHING YOU'VE EVER DREAMED OF EXISTS"

A MOMENT LATER Thurms heard the rising ghostlike echo of Bek's bellow:

"Thurms! Let us up! Don't leave us here to die."

The voice of his old commander sent Thurms into action. Making one end of the rope secure to Anar's Arch he lowered the other, shouting, "Come ahead! Bek! Can you hear me?"

"We're coming!"

The swollen sun was hanging directly over the arch like Set's heavy war mace when Bek's (naturally the first) close-cropped head emerged over the apex of the bulge. He 'walked' his way up the inclined upper half of the brow, hand over hand on the scaling rope. The first thing he said was, "Where's Tenakertom?"

Thurms pointed along the gorge. "There."

Which was enough for Bek. He took off in a determination of haste, favoring his left ankle somewhat. Thurms, watching him go, shook his head and turned back to face the great white half-circle of desert.

"Next man!" he called.

It was Hritut. He wasn't grinning. He was wet with sweat and his narrow face had an ashen hue. His eyes looked overly large in his brittle head. "Where's Bek?" he demanded. "Where has he gone?"

"On to Tenakertom."

Hritut almost looked violent. "You Maut-muddled fool, Thurms! Do you want him to find it by himself? Are you trying to *give* him the entire treasure?"

"Stop prattling like an idiot," Thurms replied. "What could he do with it if he did find it?"

Hritut tore at his corselet in a rage. "He could do too many things! Have you forgotten how he likes to play the heavy-handed army officer? He could claim it for himself! He could ambush us one by one! He could—" He broke off suddenly to glare along the deserted gorge. "That way, eh?" He unslung his bow from his shoulder and started away from Thurms on the run.

"Hritut! Wait, you fool!"

But Hritut wasn't waiting. He was going after Bek.

Kipa came up blowing and gasping and very red of face. "Thoth be praised!" he cried as he dropped the rope and grabbed for Thurms' hand. "I'm still alive!" Then he stood there wheezing and sweating and blinking around in open-mouthed bewilderment.

"But where is Tenakertom? And where are those two arch villains Bek and Hritut?"

Thurms told him, and Kipa scratched at his ears until they bled.

"Master! Master! Poor witless son of a general malady! Do you want them to rob us blind? Do you want them to steal from us that which is rightfully ours—namely the treasure? Don't you know the misbegotten rogues will turn on us at the first glint of a gold piece? Don't—"

Thurms cut the harangue short by giving Kipa a rap on his bald head.

"Kipa, control yourself. There is no need for these insane demonstrations."

"No need! No need! Did you say *no need?* You thrice-cursed product of Maut's mistake! Don't you realize that through your inept blundering you have landed us in a den of thieves? Of cutthroats?"

"Who would have cut *your* throat," Thurms interrupted, "if I had not bailed out the lot of you."

Yes, Thurms realized their position only too clearly, though he didn't see that the fault was entirely his. Things had simply worked out this way because the gods had so

directed them. Now they had to make the best of a bad slice of bread. He attempted to explain this to Kipa, but the harassed rogue had no time to waste listening to him. He had to follow Bek and Hritut. He had to seek them out and reason with them, plead with them, beg for his life (and his foolish master's too, of course), and also for a trinket or two from the treasure coffers; say three or four bags of rubies or pearls, something simple like that.

Kipa fled up the gorge in the desperate wake of the two deserters, and Thurms sighed resignedly. The climax of the venture was certainly starting off on the wrong foot—and it was a surprise to him to see Azmachis' crafty countenance emerge over the ledge of rock beaming goodnaturedly.

"Ah ha! Our friends and partners have already toddled on to the treasure city, I see."

Thurms assured him that they had indeed 'toddled on'—each one with violence and trepidation in his eye; to which Azmachis gave his soft throaty chuckle as though the fallacies of the human heart were only too well known to him.

"Typical of the lower-class Egyptian mind; greed, always greed, alas," he commented as though he alone had remained unsullied by avaricious thoughts.

"And how is it that you appear to be so calm and collected?" Thurms wondered. Azmachis smiled benignly and gave him a little pat on the shoulder.

"My son," he said paternally, "Tenakertom has waited here for seventeen hundred years. I trust it will continue to wait for a few hours more. And as for the treasure—what could one man alone do with such a hoard? Surely there is enough for all fifty times over."

"If there really is a treasure," Thurms reminded him.

A crumb of anxiety appeared in Azmachis' eye. "Y-e-s, there is always that to consider. No one, of course, knows whether or not Anar found what he was seeking on the Egma Plateau. Well, well, we've gambled this much, let us gamble the rest and press on after our dear friends."

Their 'dear friends,' Thurms was relieved to see, were not at each others' throats. They were hunkered down at the issue of the gorge gazing over at the ruined city, and at first Thurms thought it was the hoary magnitude of the crumbling pile which held them seemingly spellbound.

Tenakertom had never been a city but rather a fortress. It crouched in a wide cluster against the cliffs, huddled and decayed in two bent rows. One disorderly row of nameless rooms and a suggestion of a wall sprawled over the floor of the valley, and from this cluster the second row curved along the southern crest of the hollow. A flight of broad, patined steps lifted to a ledge and held the shattered keep. Beyond the first and lower row of building and wall was the central square. A set of cyclopean steps rose to a stone platform where the aged, weathered statue of Tanit stood.

The place fascinated Thurms as a monument to the tragedy and darkness that had fallen over this forgotten arm of entrenched early civilization. And the winds that muttered through its dusty corridors and empty rooms were the sad voices of its soldiers wailing their yesterdays into nothingness.

Without a word Thurms started forward. But Bek warned him back with a hand gesture, and pointed. "Look."

At the foot of the northeast slope, as though clinging to the ocherous rock for shelter, stood a single Arab tent. There were no camels or horses or chariots, no men or signs of men. Nothing moved except a thin twist of smoke threading up from the ragged tent into the glassy afternoon sky.

Bek was for killing whoever it was out of hand, and Hritut seconded him. Kipa wrung his hands and fumbled about his person for the elusive Thoth, and Azmachis remained strangely reticent, smiling his soft secret smile, continuing his role of the amused on-looker.

"Kemheb," Thurms breathed. Then he turned to Bek aggressively. "It must be Kemheb. And you can put all thoughts of violence out of your head. If it hadn't been for Kemheb none of us would be here. We owe him much, and there will certainly be enough to go around for one more."

Bek pulled at his nose furiously. "One more! It's always *one more!* Every time I turn around one more shows up and demands a share."

"Bek," Thurms said exasperatedly, "why don't you wait until we find the treasure before you start to worry about shares. We don't know yet if there even *is* a treasure."

It was probably the first time that Bek and Hritut had stopped to consider such a barren possibility. A look of startled concern crossed their faces, and Hritut said, "Let us hasten to the tent and wring the truth from that Set-cursed Kemheb. Surely he's been here long enough to know." Thurms caught him by the arm.

"I said no violence, Hritut. I haven't bargained for murder."

Hritut glanced at Bek, who avoided his eyes. Then he turned back and gave Thurms a sneering lop-sided smile. "Very well, son of the General. If you have assumed command here, then lead the way."

Thurms had an unhealthy feeling in his back as he started down into the green bowl. He had suddenly remembered that he no longer had his weapons—and Bek and Hritut, following closely at his heels, definitely had theirs.

The floor of the valley was grassy and strewn with curled dead leaves. They rustled in the wind like old pieces of papyrus. They blew on ahead of the little band, leading the way to the lonely tent. Thurms lifted the flap and entered. It was blue inside, shadow-blue, thick with the pungent scent of wood smoke, incense, animal skins, and other vague odors. Someone was sitting in the center of the tent. It wasn't Kemheb.

An incredibly old man, wrapped in foul linen, sat on a frayed prayer rug mumbling words that became a part of the wind and the dryly scampering leaves. A contraption like a wheel stood on a tripod at his left. It turned slowly, creaking, showing a funnel at the top and a spout at the bottom. He held a skinny claw out and let grains of sand dwindle into the mouth of the funnel. The wheel turned and other grains fell from the spout and drifted into a lacquered bowl on the rug.

A holy man, a nameless man: an Arab, a Jew, or an Egyptian. It didn't matter. Decades of a solitary, meditative wilderness existence had placed him beyond the claim or need of any given race.

Thurms spoke to him in Egyptian, and the wise man replied without looking up.

"Lay aside your weapons. You will not need them here."

Thurms glanced at Bek and Hritut. Bek was scowling at the old man, Hritut was smiling scornfully.

"There's a treasure in these ruins, isn't there?" Bek asked bluntly.

"A treasure? Yes . . . the most valuable treasure God can offer mankind." Then the old man looked at their faces. "But it won't be what you think you are looking for, and when you see it you won't recognize it . . . most of you." He lowered his head.

Thurms looked at his companions again. Hritut tapped his temple to signify madness, and Bek said harshly, "Let's get after the treasure. Leave this old fool."

"Truly," Hritut agreed. "We don't have to worry about this old goat." He and Bok pushed their way out of the tent, and Kipa paused only long enough to cast an anxious look at Thurms. Then he followed them hastily. Azmachis called to Thurms.

"Come away from here, Thurms. This man can offer you nothing."

But Thurms hesitated, held back by something intangible and mysterious. "In a moment," he said. And when he glanced over his shoulder, Azmachis had disappeared.

He stared at the old man's face, the contemplative and time-worn countenance so covered with wrinkles that it seemed to look out through the meshes of a fine dark net.

"How long have you been here, father?"

"Long . . . long . . . beyond years."

"Why?"

"To study. To think. The past is here, and the past holds the seeds of the future."

There was silence between them, disturbed only by the fitful mutter of the wind. Thurms cleared his throat.

"This *is* Tenakertom, isn't it? This is the lost city of Anar? The legend is true?"

"True—true. Anar the mighty set out with his puny legions to pit himself against a dark wilderness. Amusing, is it not? Yet many men have thought to accomplish the same impossible task, one way or another. And what does it come to in the end? Anar returned broken, dismayed, and threw up his last futile wall of defiance in this hollow of hills, and perished . . ." His voice droned on mechanically, weaving a strange hypnotic spell.

The sands dropped into the funnel, the wheel creaked, the sands drifted into the bowl.

"But he did return with a treasure, didn't he?" Thurms insisted. "Is it here?"

"He returned with nothing that was of any value to him. The treasure which is here in these ruins is a lesson that cannot be taught to blind fools."

"A lesson?"

"A lesson that teaches a truth. Go up to the scarp above the statue. You might find the answer."

Thurms moved toward the flap uneasily. When he looked back he saw the old man's bright glass-speck eyes watching him. Those eyes were like two diamonds in a mud and wattle wall.

"Four fools out of the desert," he whispered, "following a dark star—to nothing."

The tent flap fell in place and Thurms turned slowly away. Why did he say *four* fools? he wondered.

It was silent in the ruins. The murmuring wind had ceased. The dead edge-curled leaves were still. Once Thurms saw Hritut moving quickly in and out of great upreared broken blocks, searching. Bek, too, crouching before the stone arch of a green-patined tunnel, peering into the darkness beyond. He didn't see Azmachis anywhere, but Kipa was up on the elevated central square, prowling around and around the blocky pedestal of the statue of Tanit. When he spotted Thurms he began to gesticulate excitedly.

Thurms went up the cyclopean steps and crossed the dust-thick, weed-cluttered stone square. Kipa clutched for his arm, drawing him closer to the stone feet of the goddess who towered serenely above them.

"Master! Master! I do believe I have made a discovery!" Kipa slapped a stubby finger alongside his nose and winked rapidly at Thurms. "But hush, hush! Not a word to the others. Let us keep it to ourselves. Let us proceed with craft and stealth and—"

"Kipa, for Set's sake, will you collect your wits and tell me what it is you've found?"

Kipa pointed to the pedestal. Centuries of drifted sand and dirt had banked a hard cake along the sill of the limestone blocks, but Kipa had scraped away a portion of the refuse, uncovering a hand-carved inscription. Thurms squatted down before the stele block and scratched at the intricate, peculiar-looking glyphs cut into the stone with the point of his dagger.

Sunset was already in process and the light was turning against him. He was, however, certain that he made out the words *Wadi Serr* and *Akhel Foum*. He looked up at Kipa, bending eagerly over his shoulder.

"*Wadi Serr*—secret river," he said. "*Akhel Foum*—black mouth."

Kipa nodded as if he meant to shake his head loose from his neck.

"It's the rest of the Key! *I know it is!* It must be. For what other reason would those meaningless words be placed on Tanit's statue? They have nothing to do with her. They must have a purpose!"

"Perhaps so," Thurms conceded. "But there are no rivers in this valley. And Black Mouth might mean any tunnel or cave or hole in the ground."

"Stupidity!" Kipa howled. "How in the name of Maut's marvels can you be the General's son and yet remain so witless? A *see*-cret river, it says. *See*-cret! It wouldn't be rushing and rippling and flowing just *any*where! It's hidden! And I'm off to find it!"

"Very well, Kipa. But at least wait until morning. What can you hope to accomplish in the dark? You'll tumble into a pit and crack your empty head."

Kipa clawed at his face. He poured sand and dirt and salt grass over his bald head. On his knees, he stretched his arms open and raised his grimy, scratched face to Tanit, beseechingly. He demanded to know if this worthless sloth of a soldier was the same gallant adventurer who had once saved him from the teeth of a crocodile? He asked her if this lazy, befuddled youth was the same man who had sworn by Thoth to seek out and find the treasure of Tenakertom at any cost? He asked her to be kind to his master—the poor senseless bewildered boy—to watch over him while he, Kipa, the man of derring-do, set out to discover the *Wadi Serr* and the *Akhel Foum*.

Thurms threw his hands into the air in resignation and let Kipa go. Indeed, the only way to stop the fanatical fool would be to hit him over the head with a stick and tie him up with the scaling rope.

Truly, Thurms thought, *the gold bug is loose in Tenakertom.*

13

THE GOLD BUG

As though Tenakertom and its hills were sinking in the twilight sky's depth, the light lessened, darkening by shades and degrees until it transcended to a new form of illumination, as the moon—like a blind milk-white eye peering over the edge of a wall—rose above the Range, bathing the silent ruins with luminous shadows of ghostly aquamarine.

Thurms shivered as the nameless fear that sprang from the unconquered heart of Sinai tiptoed up his spine. He looked around.

A limpid mist had risen from the earth, drifting its pellucid veils in and out and among and over the old fungus-caught blocks and statues and columns and the time-worn broken bits of walls.

The treasure of Tenakertom . . . fine splendid words that slipped into a man's ears as easily as honey into the mouth. And now he, Thurms, was actually standing in the center of the lost city. And the wise man had said they wouldn't recognize the treasure when they saw it. Because it was a lesson. A lesson that taught a truth.

Azmachis had made a campfire in a nest of tumbled blocks, overlooked by a dog-face statue of Anubis, the guardian of the dead. Thurms, moody and distracted by wisps of obscure thought, walked toward the fire. The flames seemed to be battling with the murky ghost shadows of Tenakertom, like little warriors of light fighting with the giant of gloom who had his headquarters in that place.

Then Bek's disembodied call pushed back the quiet. "Hritut, you rogue! Where are you?" The only answer was a diminishing series of echoes: *areyou areyou areyou* . . .

There was nothing to eat except the dates they carried with them, plus an unrecognizable species of melon that Azmachis had discovered along the scarp that held the crumbling keep; and nothing to drink because as yet they had not found a usable well or a spring. But the melons were moist enough to satisfy thirst temporarily.

After a while Bek tramped into the circle of firelight, looking grim and belligerent, and threw himself wearily on the ground.

"Have you seen anything of that crocodile's whelp Hritut?" he demanded. And, when they told him no, he sat up to scowl suspiciously at the moony darkness.

"I don't trust him," he muttered.

"Nor do I," Azmachis hastened to assure him. "It's possible that the reason he has not returned is that he has uncovered the treasure."

The suggestion was enough for Bek. He stuffed some dates in his mouth, picked up a melon, and tramped quickly away from the fire, to become one with the night.

"Why did you tell him that?" Thurms wondered.

"Well," Azmachis said, smiling slyly, "it might be true,

you know." He gave Thurms a surreptitious glance. "What did the old man tell you?"

"Nothing that made sense. He said the treasure is a lesson that cannot be taught to blind fools. A lesson of truth; and that we might discover the answer somewhere up on the scarp above Tanit."

Azmachis pursed his pouty lips. "I wonder what he meant?"

Thurms stretched out on his back and looked up at the star-spattered sky. It was the time of night that is vast, endless, everything dead. No man's time—not belonging to the mechanism of water clocks. Cosmic night. "I wonder . . ." he murmured.

Just before he awoke he dreamed he saw horsehoofs pounding a trackless plain. The hoofs were blurred with motion and making quiet thunder in the sand and shale, reaching, throwing, going, and it seemed that he and Kemheb were back in the clattering chariot, running, always running—from what, to what? Then he was awake and half sitting up and blinking at the garlanded ruins in the dawn's lurid light, and wondering what it was that he had heard.

Azmachis was gone. Bek, Hritut, and Kipa were nowhere in sight. He sprang up, looking anxiously around. The ancient aged-in-the-stone silence of the place seemed ominous. Tenakertom seemed to be holding its breath, as though listening, waiting.

"Kipa!" he called. "Bek! Hritut?" There was no answer, only the dismal whisper of echoes. Frowning, he sliced up a melon and called it breakfast. Then he went around the square and started up the patined steps that led to the scarp ledge and the watchful keep.

The ragged ramparts of the old limestone structure had a threatening aspect, as though the wrong push here or a sudden shove there might bring the whole crumbling pile down with a crash.

A broken portal sheltered a heavy shadow pool and he stepped into it cautiously. Not only did he have to worry about the cheesy masonry overhead, but there was always the dread of unseen pitfalls underfoot. He was faced by an ancient wood-slab door that must have been a foot thick when it was first set in place. Now it was worm-riddled and moldy and as soft as corkwood. He struck it with his foot lightly and it shattered into powder and rotten splinters. The dark thick smell of dust, rot and mold touched him. He grimaced and stepped in.

The floor of the vast chamber was crisscrossed and strewn with fragments fallen from the cracked, stone-vaulted ceiling. Through the irregular breaks above, spearblades of light streamed downward, opaque and dancing with motes of dust.

He waited, letting his eyes become accustomed to the half light. When he finally took a step forward it was as if his foot had crunched through a clot of autumn leaves. He squatted down and looked closer. Then he looked out across the cluttered floor.

He was in a charnel house.

The remains of Anar's army spread before him, around him, like dry sticks, burnt scrolls, and dead leaves. Hundreds of ancient bodies in crumbling, moldy heaps; and among the litter of decayed skulls and flaking rib cages lay a hodge-podge of verdigris-coated armor—conical helmets, bronze-bladed swords, alabaster maces, flint-tipped lances, boomerangs, stone double axes, chisel-shaped arrowheads, flint knives, and shields oblong, oval, hexagonal . . . laying as though guarding their dead masters through eternity.

These were the men who had set out to conquer a dark wilderness, to rob a land of its treasures. What calamity had overtaken them? What dread plague had finally decimated the last of the Wa-shi tribe?

But it didn't matter, really. It belonged to yesterday.

Thurms straightened up and turned around and walked back through the portal, back into the clean crystalline sunlight.

He thought he was beginning to understand what the old man had meant.

All at once he stopped and looked up, breaking his muse. Bek was standing twenty paces away, half concealed behind a scrubby sidder tree, watching him, holding a nocked arrow and bow in his hands. He started bringing the bow up.

At first Thurms was certain Bek meant to kill him on the spot with the arrow; but all Bek did was make a motion with his bow for Thurms to get down. Thurms didn't waste any time about it. There was a bit of broken wall running along the edge of the ledge and he crouched behind this parapet, watching Bek all the while.

Bek seemed to be searching the lower ruins for something. His attitude gave Thurms a feeling of creeping apprehension. With an abrupt start, Bek came toward him running in a crouch. Thurms looked around for a rock, stick, anything to defend himself with.

"Have you seen that son of an ox Hritut?" Bek hunkered beside him.

"No. What has happened?"

Bek gave a grunt of grim satisfaction. "Just what I thought would happen. Hritut is going to kill us—keep the treasure for himself. That fat bandit Azmachis warned me."

Thurms stared bewilderedly. "But we haven't found a treasure—"

"Don't talk like a braying ass! It's in that old keep there. *You know it is!* That old goat in the tent told you so!" Bek peered over the edge of the parapet and pulled harshly at his nose.

"But, Bek, he didn't mean a treasure of gems and gold—"

"Close your mouth!" Bek's hard eyes flashed at him dangerously. "Don't try to trick me, Thurms. I know what's afoot. At dawn I caught Azmachis sneaking up here and I squeezed the truth out of him. He admitted that you had told him the treasure was up here—just as the old goat had informed you. But he said that Hritut had already discovered it too, and that he was hiding out and waiting to ambush the lot of us." He raised his head for another look.

"That swine! That filth of the Nile! I'll show him what it's like to come against a real soldier! He won't be the first man I've put a hole through!"

Something went *sss-wit!* over Bek's left shoulder and bounced off the limestone wall just beyond Thurms, and both of them went sprawling in the dust, face to tense face.

"Where did it come from? Could you tell?" Bek whispered.

Thurms shook his head. Bek eyed him narrowly.

"Man—where are your weapons?"

Thurms told him: bow and arrows in the desert, sword down in the gorge below Anar's Arch.

"Thurms, you stupid ox! You're less of a soldier now than when your father first sent you to the garrison at Daphnae! Well, you'll have to look to yourself. I'm not going to protect you."

He squirmed into a new position and began wiggling along the ground toward a breach in the parapet. A second arrow startled the air, going *thh-ok!* into a nearby tree. Thurms sprang up and went away running, around the backside of the old keep, hearing Hritut's distant voice roaring from somewhere.

"You marsh rats! Did you think you could trick me? Did

you think I would let you steal my treasure? By the horns of Hathor I am going to spit your bellies with arrows!"

A tumble of blocks clogged the way between the back of the keep and the sloping rise of the scarp. Thurms started to climb over and around them—only to be confronted by an apparition springing up before him. He leaped left and crouched, ready to jump again, anywhere.

It was only Azmachis; but not the Azmachis who had played the part of the reticent, smiling on-looker; nor the old obsequious, beguiling, melodramatic Azmachis. It was a cowering, trembling, scared-senseless Azmachis.

"Thurms, Thurms!" he implored, plucking at the soldier's arm. "Protect me! Hritut has gone wild with avarice and fury, because Bek tried to waylay him this morning. He means to kill all of us!"

"You don't have to tell me," Thurms said angrily, pushing the fat one away. "And he isn't alone. Bek is slightly irrational too. Why did you tell him the treasure was up here?"

"Because it's true! It's what the old man told you. And besides, I *had* to tell him something—he had a dagger at my throat!"

"Well, why did you tell him those lies about Hritut?"

"Thurms, Thurms, you poor innocent lamb! Don't you understand how dangerous those men are? I thought that if I could turn them against each other they might dispose of one another; then you and I could look for the treasure in perfect harmony and—"

"Oh, for Set's sake!" Thurms growled his disgust.

Azmachis wrung his hands. "Well, but what are we to do now, Thurms? What are we to *do?* Where have you secured your weapons? We'll need them, you know, for you to protect us."

"I haven't any weapons." Too late Thurms remembered

the old arms inside the keep. Some of the stone weapons would still be usable . . . but it wouldn't be safe to go around to the front to reach the entry portal. Anyway, there wasn't much protection in a stone axe when you were dealing with an archer who was winging arrows at you from a safe distance.

Azmachis couldn't face the bad news. He looked around at the ground frantically—presumably for something unsavory to throw in his hair. Failing in this quest, he began rending his robes, wailing:

"Then we must hide! Perhaps in a copse of wood. Perhaps in a little gorge, or even in the ruins . . . no, no, they'll be searching for each other in the ruins, and for us too . . ."

"Azmachis, try to remember that you are a Khabiri chief. Can't you retain a little dignity in an emergency?"

Obviously Azmachis couldn't. He started to make off in a hysteria of haste. Thurms caught him by the scruff of the neck, holding him back.

"We must find Kipa and warn him, and the old man too," he said.

Azmachis struggled and cursed and kicked and hit at Thurms.

"Warn them yourself! I tell you I am going to hide!"

Thurms shoved him aside with one of Set's unprintable blessings. He picked a path through the block tumble and found an old stone gutter or drain that sloped down into the bowl's center. The run of concave-shaped stones was verdure-clad and bordered on either side with ferns. He made his way down the golden moss-soft shoot unobserved and crept into the main cluster of the lower ruins.

Moving among the debris, shifting rapidly from one upreared broken block to the next, he threaded his way through grass-choked courts and along rows of sculptured pillars, ornate from pedestal to capital—many of them down like wind-felled timber; passing in and out of empty chambers, each one surely the drab home of some blind soul of loneliness . . . until finally he found himself standing in the inner shrine of an old temple.

Glancing around he saw that it was the ruined fane of Isis, the wife and sister of Osiris. The goddess, with her lotus-shaped head and the sistrum in her hand, stared at him with pleasant, stone-blind eyes. She was no help to him at all.

Right beside the larger-than-life statue was a portal leading to yet another pillared court, and he took it because it lay in the general direction he wanted to go—back to the Arabian tent. He stepped into a large chamber that still bore a fair share of its crackling roof, making the old room weirdly crepuscular and indistinct.

The moment he stepped through the doorway he received an intangible premonition of danger, the sense of an imperative presence that was unseen and hostile and right behind him. He heard it let out its breath.

Then he jumped, to the left, and a second later would have been too late. A two-handed sword went *wwwhisk,* sweeping downward and back into the shadows, and he spun about and had just one quick glimpse of Hritut's stark eyes, bared lips, and clenched teeth. He straight-armed the deserter away from him and sprang back through the doorway. He grabbed the tall stone statue and lunged with it, tipping it off balance, and lunged again and tilted it slantwise across the doorway, the lotus-shaped head jamming in the upper right angle, and he braced himself against it, arms and legs, holding it in place.

He felt it shove from the other side; then he heard Hritut bellow with rage. There were no words to the man's harangue, only insane sound rising and falling with his labored breathing.

The trouble was the tilted statue left wide, irregular openings on either side, and now Hritut was trying to get his arm and sword through one of them to take a swing at Thurms.

Suddenly he heard the scuff-scuffing of sandals coming from behind, and he turned his head and was appalled to see fat Kipa waddling toward him in a businesslike stride.

"Master, Master! A great discovery! I have—" He stopped by one of the ornate pillars and looked at Thurms with widening eyes.

"Whatever on earth are you attempting to do with Isis? Don't you know it's bad luck to knock a god about in that unruly manner?"

"Run for cover, Kipa! Quick!"

A foot of bronze blade glinted around the sistrum Isis was holding, and Thurms jerked his head aside to escape the slash that was aimed at his face. Kipa dropped his lower jaw and his tongue nearly spilled out of his mouth.

"For Set's sake, will you run!" Thurms cried. "I can't hold him!"

The swordblade chopped again and went *clock!* against the sistrum and stone splinters flew into the air. Thurms ducked, flinging his body back, but held on. He glanced toward the pillar where the startled Kipa had been standing. Good, he was gone.

A crash, and chips of stone pitted his face. The swordblade withdrew and Hritut's grimaced face showed briefly in the slot. His eyes glowed madly at Thurms, then winked away. Thurms heard him take a deep intake of breath and he knew that this time Hritut was going to do his utmost to slash him.

He released the statue and sprang backwards as Hritut's sword, arm, and left shoulder emerged from the slot and hacked at him. He pivoted and went across the fane in a run, hearing the temple-trembling crash of the stone Isis behind him. Hritut yelled something but it was only gibberish to Thurms. He crossed a great chamber that had many wings opening behind it, and one of them led to a series of open courtyards.

He started toward them, then stalled. No, that wouldn't do. If he went outside he would just keep running—like Kipa and Azmachis. And the only thing running ever proved was that you were afraid to face a crisis. Something had to be done about Hritut and Bek—something, he didn't know what, but something.

He entered a broad, short passageway. It was floored with broken tiles and the old stained limestone walls bore pictures of men and beasts. It was vaulted overhead, dark. And there was a noise that his intelligence couldn't pinpoint at first; a running, murmuring, smothering noise of . . . *Water,* he said. He peered down at the dimness underfoot. He had approached the lip of a ledge. It was set in the center of the wide passage and it was a circular shaft. Cautiously, he looked over the edge.

Forty feet down his eye caught the dark motion of sliding water.

A well . . . a well sunk in the heart of Tenakertom to a subterranean river. *Wadi Serr,* the secret river.

The passage that contained the well was set in a thick wall between two adjoining chambers. It was about fifteen feet long. There was a narrow runway on either side of the well and he took the one on his right hand, moving with his back against the wall. He stopped halfway and stared suspiciously at the archway to the next chamber. It was suddenly very quiet in the temple, and he wondered where Hritut was.

He wiped at his face, at the nervous sweat in his eyes. He looked at his hands, empty, and wished for a weapon. Then he started again.

Quite distinctly he heard the scuff of a sandal on the grit of the tile flooring. He froze and sucked in his breath. A sandal moved once on the tile in the chamber behind him. Then, nothing. He put a hand to his stomach and gripped the flesh hard, tried to make a tight ball of it. Something—he couldn't tell where—made a creak, and again, nothing. He let his breath out slowly.

How did the sun set? Would he be able to pick up a shadow through the light of the broken roof when Hritut came across the rear chamber? Would he come that way? Madmen, he knew, could be very crafty.

Suppose now, Hritut had not come all the way into the rear chamber. What if he had found another passage to the adjoining room and had sneaked through it and around to the other archway of the . . .

He heard breathing—hesitant, secret breathing.

Thurms whipped about. Too late—the sword glinted over

his head, flashed down. *"YAH!"* Hritut's mouth screamed out of the gloom.

Thurms wrenched his head to one side, knocking it violently against the wall, and felt the blade nick into his right shoulder, heard the *daank!* as it struck stone, and almost instantly the passageway resounded with a scream that seemed to draw down down down as Thurms clung to the dark fungus-damp wall, his equilibrium completely out of tilt.

EEEEEEeeeeee— Spaasssh!

Thurms got out of there, dazedly. Hritut had just taken the longest trip in his life. He had struck, missed, lost his balance, and now he belonged to the *Wadi Serr*.

14

THE BLACK MOUTH

THE SUNLIGHT was clear, strong, beautiful. Thurms walked through it, across the weedy old courtyards, gratefully. Then he looked up at the scarp and saw Kipa and Azmachis standing together on the ramp. Wordlessly they were rending their garments and he could see at a glance that they were scared to death. Then he saw why.

The burly, iron-eyed Bek was standing to one side of them with an arrow nocked in his bow.

"Where's that dog of the delta Hritut?" he called. And, when Thurms told him, he cried, "Hi! There's a well-deserved death! Very well, Thurms, come up here. Quick now!"

Thurms came up the steps of the ramp and glanced uneasily at Kipa and Azmachis. They had nothing to say. They appeared—for the first time in their colorful lives—to be totally cowed. Evidently Bek had been intimidating them. Bek made a motion with his bow.

"Now, let's get on to the treasure! The old goat said it was in this keep."

"What treasure?" Thurms said. "There's only bones and dust in there."

Bek wasn't having any of that. His eyes turned bright and mean, glinting like two little specks of glass in the hot sun. "Don't try to serve me that bones-and-dust rubbish! I *know* the treasure is there!" He jabbed at Thurms with the tip of the bronze arrowhead. "Move along!"

Bek was the great leader again, the conquering warrior. It was, Thurms realized, no time for an argument. He turned and led the way into the crumbling keep, Kipa and Azmachis crowding up fearfully at his back, Azmachis whispering huskily, "He's mad, gold mad!"

Bek herded them away from the broken doorway, ordering them into the center of the huge chamber where he could keep an eye on them. Then he looked down at the ghastly cluttered floor—and began to giggle and shiver.

"Gold, Thurms! Gold and jewels! A roomful of it! Treasure!"

He dropped to hands and knees among the filth, dust, bones and old old rubble. He chortled crazily.

Thurms watched him, appalled. "Bek, there is no treasure here. No gold, no—"

"*You lie!*" Bek screamed, and he pivoted about—still on his knees—and leveled the bow at Thurms. "I know you, Thurms. You want my treasure. You're like Hritut. Well, do you know what you are going to get it its place, my little general's son? An arrow!"

Kipa's pudgy hands were fumbling over his garments as though seeking new places to tear and rend, but Thurms had forgotten just how talented those hands were. Like the snap of fingers Thoth, all black and long and tail cocked, appeared in Kipa's right hand and he flipped the ghastly thing at Bek's face, calling:

"Catch!"

A cry strangled in Bek's throat as he frantically threw up his arms and the bow to ward off the scorpion. The bowstring went *twamp!* as the arrow zipped upward into the stone-vaulted roof overhead. Thurms took one quick long step forward, swung an unconsciously directed uppercut at the point of Bek's chin, and Bek's head snapped back and he went over and down.

The neat blow had been about three thousand years ahead of its time but none of them could realize it at that moment; in fact, they didn't even stop to think about it at all. Azmachis sank into the filth with a hearty sigh of relief, and Kipa chased after Thoth who was angry at being tossed about like a beanbag, and Thurms lashed Bek's hands with Bek's belt and his feet with his own belt.

"Thoth, you are truly a god of gods!" Kipa complimented his little friend.

Thurms and Kipa supporting the unconscious Bek, Azmachis leading the way, they went down to the central square and placed Bek in the shade at Tanit's stone feet. Then Thurms, straightening up to wipe his brow, glanced around and saw Azmachis moving slowly, heavily away from them. He was heading toward the pass to Anar's Arch.

"Azmachis! Where are you going?"

Kipa tugged entreatingly at Thurms' arm. "Let him go. Let him go. We don't want him. I've made an important discovery while you were playing hide and seek with the others."

Thurms shrugged him off and went after Azmachis in a trot.

"Azmachis! What are you doing?"

Wearily, bleak-faced, the Khabiri chief turned and looked at Thurms.

"I'm going home, Thurms."

"Home? Now?"

Azmachis nodded. "I've been a fool. I've been chasing after a child's dream. There is no treasure here—only ruins and decay. I curse the day I encountered Kemheb! I first went to Tanis as a spy, to determine the Egyptian fortifications and strength. Until I met Kemheb I believed in the Khabiri cause; after I met him I forgot about the Khabiri, about my own people. All I could think of was the gold of Tenakertom. After my—shall I say—bodyguard died in the desert, I went on alone, hoping to talk my way out of danger. I saw the death trap and walked right into it." He sighed and shifted his eyes over the silent ruins.

"And what have all my machinations led to? Lust and greed and violence. Hritut dead and Bek insane. And all for nothing. No, I have come to my senses at last. I am done with it."

"Well," Thurms said inadequately, "well—"

"Farewell, Thurms. You may not be the greatest soldier Egypt has ever produced, but you are the best embodiment of youth I've ever encountered. I envy you."

And so, perhaps, unconsciously, Azmachis too had learned the Lesson.

Kipa was all in a dither over his discovery. Impatiently he led Thurms to the northeast oval of the valley and pointed to a green-walled canyon that lay like a crack in the slope. "Listen!" he commanded, cocking his head to one side.

A sound came out of the ground—a faint droning sound like the noise that might be made by a distant squadron of chariots rumbling over a stony plain. Thurms looked at Kipa, who was holding his finger to the side of his nose and winking rapidly at him.

"The subterranean river," Thurms whispered. *"Wadi Serr."*

Kipa nodded vigorously and pointed up the gorge. "You can hear it all the way up this canyon!"

So this is what must have happened: in an earlier time a river had cut through this canyon and made a lake of the bowl where the ruins of Tenakertom now stood. The overspill had gone under Anar's Arch and caused a waterfall into the hollow below the stone wall, and then cut out the gorge to the oasis and desert beyond. But somehow, Thurms reasoned, the river had been diverted, swung into a new bed and gone underground.

None of this interested Kipa, however. He was in a hot sweat to follow the *Wadi Serr* to its source.

"You mean to say you haven't gone up the canyon yet?" Thurms asked. And Kipa became greatly flustered and glanced around uneasily.

"We-ll, not *all* the way," he confessed. "There's something in the canyon that made me think perhaps I had better wait until you were along. Come, I will show you."

The canyon, fern walled and fern roofed, garlanded with wild flowers and sparkling moss, became more and more tunnel-like. Abruptly Kipa stopped and pointed. An old square of limestone had been set into the canyon wall on the right-hand side. It was a stele, bearing on its smooth surface a row of barely discernible letters. The inscribed message was in early Egyptian.

> This is Tanit's warning to the stranger: if you are weary of life, keep on walking up this canyon. If you come as a friend seeking friends, beware just the same.

Kipa fussed nervously with his robes.

"It—uh isn't a very promising welcome, is it?"

If you come as a friend seeking friends, Thurms thought, and he felt a sensation—a tingling of the kind that goes leaching over bare skin like cold water on a hot day.

"We've come this far," he said, "and we're not going to be turned back now by an ancient inscription written for the superstitious. Onward, brave Kipa! Think of the treasure!"

Brave Kipa thought of the treasure and muttered, "Yes, onward," weakly.

They pushed on up the green-crowding gorge, coming at last to the end, and stepped quietly into a sun pool. All around them, the dark walls of rock rose like great black statues, and the sun's glancing rays seemed to knock sparks out of the basalt.

A tomb chapel had been built in a small setback in the rocks. Its columned portico was built of limestone blocks and it was surmounted by a small pyramid of brick which had once been covered with stucco and capped by a granite pyramidion. In the shadows of the porch was a stele and two funerary statues—lifelike man statues of a general.

A slim, tanned, ragged youth squatted in the weed-grown court before the chapel, holding a bit of meat on a stick over a small fire.

"Kemheb," Thurms said.

Kemheb sprang to his feet, dropping the stick and meat. His teeth flashed in a grin as he cried, "Thurms! I knew you would come!"

They gripped hands and for a long wordless minute they simply stood there looking at each other, grinning like two fools, while Kipa tugged at his ears and hopped from one foot to the other, muttering, "But the treasure! What about the treasure? Is this the Black Mouth?"

Finally Kemheb turned to the impatient rogue and said no. The Black Mouth was inside the tomb, and the interior tomb had been hewn out of the living rock.

"Then you haven't found the treasure?" Kipa asked urgently.

Kemheb shook his head. "I haven't been here long myself. And it took me Set's own time to get as far as I've come. I lost your team and chariot in the desert, Thurms, and it then took me two weeks to locate Seken's Well after I finally reached the oasis."

"How did you manage to pass the wall under Anar's Arch?"

"Scaled it," Kemheb said simply. Thurms looked at his young friend with silent admiration. Seemingly nothing could stop this wiry youth from obtaining his goal.

Kipa was beside himself with anxiety. "Yes, yes. But if you had discovered the Secret River and tracked it to this hidden tomb, and there found the Black Mouth, why in Maut's marvelous name haven't you found the treasure?"

Kemheb's smooth brow wrinkled. "There are complications," he explained. "The Wa-shi vaulted the interior of the tomb with limestone blocks, but with the passing of the centuries—and due to the constant vibration of the *Wadi Serr* undermining the tomb—there have been repeated cave-ins. I have had to work with extreme care in removing the rubble for fear of suddenly causing another avalanche."

"Never mind about such trifles," Kipa cried. "Let us hasten on to the treasure!"

Thurms winked at Kemheb. "Let us get on with the business, before Kipa goes mad and starts biting his tail like a dog."

Arming themselves with firebrands the three adventurers entered the antechamber of the tomb. It was a crazyhouse of piled limestone blocks, great craggy chunks of rock, rotting timbers, and a mass of dusty, decaying boxes, vases, statues, and tomb furniture. The vaulted ceiling overhead loomed high and forbidding, dancing now with orange and brown shadows from the smoking torches. Kemheb silently pointed out a toppled stele. The old inscription read:

Anar, thy mummy-shell is of gold, with head of lapis lazuli; the cover is over thee and thou art placed upon a sledge. Oxen drag thee and the dance of the Muu is performed for thee at the door of the tomb.

Thurms looked up at Kemheb. "Anar's tomb," he whispered. And Kemheb nodded. Silently now, they picked their way over the rubble to a stairwell dug in the rock. Most of the well was clogged with a jumble of stones, but Thurms could see the upper half of a black plastered archway. Set inside the recess of the arch was a sealed door. He looked at Kemheb, and the youth nodded again.

"The Black Mouth."

Thurms led the way down the steps and over the stones. Once Kipa stumbled and a clutter of blocks caused a minor landslide. Instantly a tremulous crackling came down from the upper reaches of the stony ceiling. The three adventurers caught their breath, staring at each other fixedly, waiting. Nothing more happened.

"Can't you be careful?" Thurms hissed at Kipa. "Do you want to crush us to death?"

"Is it my fault if Anar's slothful slaves constructed his tomb out of rotting cheese?" Kipa retorted testily.

'Rotting cheese' was an apt term. Time and the vibrations of the *Wadi Serr* were pulling apart the mighty hewn stones of the tomb. With extreme care they started to work clearing the rubble from the sunken archway, handing up the chunks and shards of stone one by one. It was like working in a small closed closet on a summer day. And what little air there was was foul. And all the while the rumble of the hidden river beat in their ears and slopped and slushed around in their brains like warm heady wine.

But it was finished at last, and without mishap. Sweat-blinded, taking quick gulps of the humid air, they paused and rested; then—in silent, common agreement—went to work on the heavily plastered door, Thurms using Bek's sword, Kemheb a javelin he had saved from the chariot, and Kipa a bronze chisel he had found in the antechamber.

They broke the necropolis seal—clear proof that a person of high standing was interred within. Slowly the old heavy door cracked open. The torches fluttered and faltered as a thick miasmic air came at them, and the three adventurers had to flee to the upper chapel.

"Did you see anything?" Kemheb asked eagerly. Thurms shook his head. He was too excited to speak.

The air seemed better when they descended the steps the second time and looked at the Black Mouth and hesitated. The archway spat fear at them like a cobra spitting poison—a fear that got into the blood. Thurms shoved the door wider. The torchlight leaped into a chamber 25 ft by 15 ft, and the dog-headed god Anubis seemed to rear itself out of the darkness as if startled by their approach. He stared at them blankly with his dusty jeweled eyes.

A clutter of alabaster vases and ship models stood around two statues of guardian gods, armed with maces and staffs and with protective sacred cobras upon their foreheads.

The shadows of weird animal heads danced on the walls. Little effigies of servants of the dead to do the General's will in the afterworld stood by a richly decorated shrine. There was a golden throne, a chariot, a hunting bow and javelin, and a large model palace made of calcite. The seeking torchlight spread over the great sarcophagus, made from a single block of yellow quartzite with a rose granite lid.

Anar's mummy would be inside. But they had no desire to see it, or to disturb the General in his eternal sleep.

The light bit at something that sparkled with a deep crimson hue. An overturned alabaster vase had spilled out a pool of rubies. Kipa gave a strangled cry and rushed to the treasure, dropping to his knees he dug his hands into the glowing gems. *"Mine! Mine! Mine!"* he crowed, and he began stuffing them into his capacious pockets and inside his robes and garments—undoubtedly to the consternation of Thoth.

Kemheb and Thurms made no move. They simply stood and stared as though bemused. When Kemheb spoke it was in a low voice, as if afraid of the mocking echoes in the roof of the place.

"Ah—thus ends a Dynasty." He sounded a little sad.

Thurms said nothing. He was thinking that the treasure of Tenakertom had not been one of gold and jewels after all. There was gold, of course, but most of it was in large carved forms and would be bulky and awkward to transport. Who would care to try to carry a golden throne across the desert of Sinai? And though Kipa had uncovered a vase of rubies, Thurms nowhere saw the vast quantities of priceless gems he had expected to see. Yet, somehow, he wasn't disappointed.

He knew now that adventure for monetary gain was merely stupid, that adventure in itself was useless hardship unless a man seeks some selfless principle. Kemheb, with his remarkable insight, seemed to divine his thoughts.

"It is fitting that we leave Anar now in this place that is proper for him to be—in the tomb of lost dreams. We have disturbed him, yet I doubt that he really minds. For someone at last has now established him as a man. Anar and his Tenakertom are no longer mere myths."

Thurms nodded. It was enough. He was satisfied. He had found what he had come to find, seen what he had needed to see. It was time to go.

"Come away from that, Kipa," he ordered. "We are leaving."

Kipa couldn't believe the announcement. "Leaving? *Leaving!* Are you mad? We haven't found the treasure! Merely a few baubles. We must press on with our search! There are bound to be other adjoining chambers. Treasure chambers! We will tear the walls apart! We wi—"

Thurms and Kemheb had to drag him away from his pool of rubies, Kipa fighting them tooth and nail, kicking and screaming and clutching at the statue of Anubis, then at the crumbling plastered door, then at the jamb of the doorway itself.

"Look out!" Kemheb suddenly cried.

An abrupt gut-grabbing crackling overhead gave swift point to his cry. Terror sprang upon Thurms and he shoved the fat Kipa full-length through the door and went after him in a toppling heap, hearing Kemheb shout from somewhere.

"Up! Up! Quick! Run!"

Thurms shoved up in a tangle of legs and arms and

grabbed at Kipa and together they blundered up the now dark steps, as the massive lintel beam of tamarisk wood which had upheld the archway for seventeen hundred years, gave again with a loud *skraack!* and shattered. The great limestone blocks above it came smashing down in a smoking dust cloud.

They were in the upper antechamber now and running, leaping over the rubble-strewn way toward the distant rectangle of daylight glowing through the outer chapel door, while above them came the giving roar of more great stones as the whole roof of the tomb, formed by overlapping courses of masonry crowned by hewn capstones, fell in.

Something—heavy, quick, inexorable as the hand of Set—struck Thurms a glancing blow on the back and sent him spinning through the doorway and under the crumbling portico. Then Kemheb had him by one arm and was dragging him clear, and it sounded as if the whole world were coming asunder behind him.

"Kipa!" he yelled. "Where's Kipa?"

"Right here by your side, good kind brave master! Right where your faithful servant should be," the rogue said with a sort of half hopeful, half sheepish smile.

"Kipa—!" Thurms started to berate the fat greedy fool, but shut up before he could get started. After all, a friend was a friend; you had to accept his bad habits along with his good. He was grateful that Kipa was still alive. "—How is Thoth?" he finished lamely.

"He's playing with the rubies I've given him, Master. He's as happy as a god or mortal could hope to be."

Bek was conscious but not himself. He whined and complained that he wanted to go back up to the keep and see his 'treasure' again. Kipa promised to give him some nice old bones to play with later on if he would behave himself. Thurms felt sorry for the commander. He'd been a good soldier in his day.

"We can lower him down the stone face by the rope," Kemheb said.

Thurms nodded. "We'll keep him in the chariot. One of us will steer and the other two will walk. We'll switch around every few miles. That way we should be able to carry enough water and fodder to see us to Fort Harba." But he wasn't ready to leave Tenakertom yet.

"One moment. I want to see the old man again."

"Why, for Ammon's sake?" Kipa demanded.

"Because he said something when we first talked to him that puzzled me. He said '—the most valuable treasure *God* can offer mankind.' He didn't say Aton or Ammon or any of the others, nor did he say *the gods*. He simply said God."

"A slip of the tongue," Kipa declared.

"Perhaps. But I made the same slip when I was ready to fall from Anar's Arch—and I didn't fall."

"It's a waste of time," Kipa insisted. "The old fool doesn't know anything. He was wrong about the treasure, wasn't he?"

"No," Thurms said, thinking about the Lesson. "He was right."

The old man still sat in the blue scented shadows of his tent. The wheel had almost stopped turning. A sand grain drifted into the lacquered bowl. Thurms thought he was asleep, but he stirred and spoke without looking up.

"The sands are running out," he whispered.

Thurms didn't know what to say. The possibility that the old man had come to Tenakertom to die had suddenly struck him. Finally he asked, "I want to know if Aton is a true god?"

"Aton?" The old man seemed to be tasting the name. "Aton?"

"He is an Egyptian god our Pharaoh introduced. He is called the only god and he created all things. He is without form and he says that all men—slave and Pharaoh alike—are equal."

The old man nodded, and when he spoke he said his words quietly, without inflection, letting them dribble like grains of sand on a beach.

"Yes, that is true. There is only one God, though His name is not Aton. Your Pharaoh is obviously a man of great prescience . . . but unfortunately he is ahead of his time. Mankind is not yet ready to understand the marvels of God."

"You mean to say that Aton will fail?"

A ghost of a smile flittered across the old man's lips at the use of the name Aton. "God never fails, only man. He will come when the time is right, though it may take a millennium—"

"A thousand years?" Thurms cried.

"Perhaps longer. Time is relative only to man. In the scheme of things, as in space, time is timeless and a millennium may be tomorrow. And this time when He comes He will remain forever, and His appearance will not be far from here. There is a little walled city in Syria, and there . . ." He stopped, like a clepsydra that had run out of water, caught in introspection.

For an immeasurable moment they remained in place: the tall young soldier and the old bent soothsayer, one standing and one sitting, in the scented blue-shadowed tent, as intangible visions of the future came up and snuffled around Thurms' feet.

"Farewell, father," he murmured.

"Farewell, Thurms."

It was only later, as Kipa and Kemheb were helping Bek through the gorge to Anar's Arch, that Thurms suddenly stopped to ask himself a moot question. *How could he have possibly known my name?*

15

FOLLOW THE DARK STAR

Senmut had regained his reason as well as his command of Fort Harba. He detailed a squad of men to take charge of the mumbling Bek, and he took Thurms, Kemheb and Kipa to his quarters and served them wine and food. He was exuberant and healthy—a new man.

"The war is as good as over," he informed them. "Horemheb had his hour, and he is now out mopping up the last of the Khabiri—chasing them back to their foothills where they belong. Believe me, my friends, Horemheb gave them a drubbing they will not soon forget!"

"But how?" Thurms wondered. "When he was so heavily outnumbered?"

It seemed that when Horemheb had lost his advantage of having the Khabiri on the run, the Khabiri had turned back en masse and had decided to attack the Egyptians. Horemheb's little army had been caught in the open desert.

Horemheb had quickly set his men to work at digging a series of deep trenches, to setting up stones, to driving stakes between the stones, to stretching rush ropes between the stakes, constructing a barricade that would prove fatal to charging teams and chariots. This obstacle trap was his introductory barricade. Behind his own troops he dug the longest, deepest trench of all and covered it over with karoo bushes. Then the Egyptians waited for the Khabiri hordes.

At dawn the Khabiri formed their chariots in battle order, then sent out single riders on fast horses. The riders bucked their mounts on on on, themselves leaning over to one side with swords in their right hands to cut away the rush ropes of the barricade, but picking only certain spots in the long obstacle front. Then other riders followed them into these breaches and flung pennant-butted spears upright in the ground. Then all of them, swordmen and spearmen, went booting out of there followed by a hail of Egyptian arrows.

Horemheb, wise in the ways of war, instantly understood what the tribesmen were up to. "On your feet, you marsh rats of Egypt!" he ordered his men. "Those flagged spears are meant to mark the breaches in our defense, to guide the Khabiri chariots through the barricades. Now get out there and move the spears to portions of the barricade that are still unbreached!"

This was quickly done, and just in time, for like the wrath of Set and all his scurvy minions the Khabiri squadrons came thundering down on the Egyptian defense. But the barricade held and the chariots and teams and Khabiri themselves were thrown against the stones and ropes and trenches and peppered with arrows and javelins and stopped cold.

Horemheb was everywhere, racing back and forth behind his line in his fast, light chariot, berating his soldiers in a roaring voice, calling them 'Delta beetles' and 'Carrion eaters' and 'Maut's mistakes,' telling them they were 'gutless' and 'aimless,' declaring that they didn't have the spunk to stand up to a broken-legged Khabiri midwife and that they couldn't hit the side of a fort with an arrow if they stood beside the wall and tossed arrows at it ten at a time, and—furthermore—that Ammon must surely be hiding his face in shame when he saw how the 'rats of the Nile' were disgracing the fair name of Egypt by their craven, slothful impersonation of soldiers.

And they loved him for it. Every 'marsh rat' in the fighting line cheered as he went clattering by, insulting them in his brawling battlefield voice.

And they fought for him as they had never fought before. And they died for him gladly, as though he had blessed them instead of berated them. And they beat back the Khabiri chariots three times.

Yet each time the Khabiri charged they cleared a wider path for the heavy war chariots that were yet to come, and every professional soldier in the Egyptian line could see that before long the barricade would be breached completely.

Now the fighting turned to hand-to-hand, with the Egyptians wading into the tangle of downed horses and overturned chariots, and lunged with their spears at the oncoming charioteers and brought the horses down with snares and filled the air with the *twa-twa-twa-twamp* of their bowstrings, while the whirling copper blades on the Khabiri chariot wheels went *knack-knack-knack* as they cut through the din.

Then it was the time for the fourth charge, when the Khabiri were ready to unleash their heavy war chariots. Leaving only a token line of infantry defense behind the barricade, Horemheb pulled his main army back into the sand hills and let the Khabiri roll on.

They came like Set's thunderbolt, like the end of the earth in one great slamming banging screaming splash. They tore through the twisted carnage of the previous charges, rocking over the stones and bouncing over the clogged pits and passing through the severed ropes and overran the thin line of Egyptian infantry, then went crashing into the clearing behind the barricade screaming their triumphant war cry—*Ul-ul-ul-ul-ullah!* and directed their careening chariots toward the long row of karoo bushes which fronted the Egyptian-held hills.

"Listen," Senmut said with great agitation. "The sight which we next beheld will live with me till the day I step into Ammon's golden boat! Picture it! Horses, chariots, drivers, archers, all piling wheels over hoofs into this great pit! And then, before they could regain their senses, we poured a murderous rain of arrows, spears and javelins down on their tangled mass from our hills. Within the space of fifteen minutes we had completely annihilated their squadron of war chariots!"

After that Horemheb had turned his own chariot squadron loose on the Khabiri foot army, and this time the panic that overtook the tribesmen was a lasting terror and they fled into the desert with Horemheb hot on their sandy heels.

Leaving the demented Bek in Senmut's charge, Thurms and Kemheb decided to press after Horemheb's army. But Kipa (now that he was the richest man in Sinai) elected to remain at Harba until a passing caravan came his way. He then planned on purchasing the caravan and having it conduct him back to Tanis in great state; there he would buy up land and have a palace constructed for himself and, perhaps, even a pyramid in the event of his death—which event he sincerely trusted and hoped would be far far in the future.

"If you ever find yourself in the vicinity of my palace, come and visit with me and Thoth," he invited Thurms, loftily. "I shall always hold a soft spot in my great heart for old comrades."

"Kipa, Kipa, you old rogue." Thurms could not conceal his amusement over Kipa's pomposity. "Don't you know that through your foolishness and extravagance you will have squandered your rubies before a year is out? What will you do then?"

"What matter?" Kipa said airily. "I shall always know where to go for more." Then he sobered enough to return to earth, placing his finger alongside his nose and giving Thurms a slyly hopeful look.

"But—uh, Thurms, master—in the event of such an emergency may I count upon you to—uh help me make another expedition to Tenakertom?"

Thurms laughed and clapped him on the shoulder. "Kipa, I readily believe that it is written in the sands that we shall indeed meet again. But I greatly doubt that it will be on the track to Tenakertom. Farewell, 'faithful servant.' Remember me to Thoth!"

It took Thurms and Kemheb two days to catch up to Horemheb, and when they did it was at night and the Egyptian army was scattered over the surrounding dunes, their pinpoints of little cookfires glowing like clusters of Kipa's rubies against the vast black backdrop of the Sinai night. Horemheb was sitting on the sand with his back to a chariot wheel, eating bread and onions with his staff officers. In the firelight he looked gaunt and tired, but as indomitable as ever.

He looked up at Thurms and spat a bit of onion skin from his mouth and jerked a wolf's grin over his adamant-like face.

"Ammon kick us! This boy appears at my elbow every time I've reached the decision to inform his father of his death! Well, Thurms, did you find Bek?"

"Yes sir. Senmut has him under restraint at Harba. He—isn't quite himself."

"Desert madness, eh?"

"Y-e-s, a form of madness," Thurms admitted.

Horemheb kept sending sharp glances at Kemheb, but continued to address his questions to Thurms.

"And this Tenakertom—did you find that as well?"

"Yes sir, we did."

"Hmm. And the treasure?"

Thurms decided that Horemheb would be the last man in the world to understand the real treasure of Tenakertom—the Lesson of the great dead army in the crumbling old keep.

"No sir. At least not one that could be transported across the burning desert. We discovered Anar's tomb."

Horemheb didn't care a Syrian jar about Anar's tomb. Anar was a dead general. Horemheb was a very much alive general. He turned his blue-chipped gaze on Kemheb again and this time he frowned openly.

"Don't I know you from somewhere, boy? Step more into the light."

"This is Kemheb, sir. The slave who held the Key to Tenakertom," Thurms explained.

Horemheb's brow made a tight V. "Kemheb—Kemheb," he muttered, as though annoyed by a fluke of memory. Suddenly his look brightened and he pointed a commanding finger at the slim, silent youth.

"In Thebes. Yes! I've seen you in Pharaoh's Golden House in Thebes. Aren't you Kemhotep, Tutankhamon's cousin—a member of the royal family?"

Kemheb gave Thurms a worried glance and lowered his head. He nodded grudgingly. "A distant member of the royal family," he admitted. "Tutankhamon is my second cousin."

Thurms couldn't believe what he was hearing. He literally

gawked at Kemheb. And the collection of silent staff officers were nearly doing the same thing. Even Horemheb was watching Kemheb with a peculiar expression.

"Tutankhamon is Pharaoh of Egypt," Horemheb said quietly.

"*Tut?*" Both Thurms and Kemheb were startled. Horemheb nodded.

"Pharaoh Akhnaton is dead. Sekenre, his oldest son-in-law, would have been Pharaoh but he had a foolish accident on the Nile only a few days after Akhnaton's death and drowned himself. And so—King Tut."

Thurms and Kemheb were stunned by the news. Tut—king of Egypt! Surely the gods must be having their little joke.

Horemheb shifted his sharp gaze back to Thurms. "Well, Thurms, it appears that your father and I were wrong in our estimation of you."

"I don't understand, sir."

"It's quite simple," Horemheb said. "You didn't save a slave boy from the Khabiri: you saved the life of Pharaoh's cousin."

"He saved me twice, General," Kemheb stated. "I was trapped at Tenakertom without a team and chariot."

Horemheb grunted. "It seems we'll have to give Thurms an advancement after all." He thought for a moment, then turned to Kemheb. "I'll arrange an escort to return you safely to Thebes. Thurms will be in charge of the party, with a captain's rank."

Thurms and Kemheb both thanked the General and started to turn away, but Thurms hesitated.

"Sir, now that Tut is Pharaoh—what has become of Aton?"

Horemheb reached for another onion. "Aton is finished," he said flatly. "Tut has declared Aton a false god and thrown him out of Egypt. He plans to reinstate Ammon as the 'all powerful.' "

It was a blow to Thurms. For some reason Aton had come to mean something to him. Now he was gone. Horemheb, watching him, said:

"Cheer up, Thurms. Gods come and go, just as men do. Some good, some bad. Aton had his day, and now it's over. Forget it."

Yes, Thurms thought with a sudden uplift of spirit. *But he'll have his day again.*

From the top of the highest sand dune, with the cookfires of the army at their backs, Thurms and Kemheb stood side by side and contemplated the far-spreading, star-struck desert of Sinai before them.

Finally Thurms turned to Kemheb. "Why did you keep your identity from me? You would let me think you were a slave—had I been witless enough to be deceived."

" 'It is a soldier's duty to protect all Egyptians—slaves or not,' " Kemheb quoted Thurms with a grin. "But would you have believed me that first day if I had told you that I was Tut's cousin?"

Thurms had to admit that he probably would not. Kemheb nodded.

"Anyway, I would rather be Kemheb the explorer than Kemhotep the cousin of Pharaoh Tutankhamon."

"Yes," Thurms said unhappily, "but now you will be returned to Thebes to live in the Golden House with the royal family."

Kemheb looked as glum about it as Thurms did.

"And what of yourself, Thurms? Now that you've risen in rank I suppose you'll stay in the army. Your father will probably appoint you a position in the royal household guard at Thebes."

Thebes—the city of his birth; the most wonderful city in all the world. Yet, somehow, it no longer seemed to mean as much to him as it once did. He felt the sensation of a loss, as if something had dropped out of his life, spilled away in the sands around his feet.

Kemheb was studying him in the dark. "Thurms," he said, and a note of urgency had entered his voice, "when the nomadic Hyksos invaders were driven from Egypt 200 years ago, they made their last stand somewhere along the desert border between Sinai and Syria. It is thought that they built a fort called Sharuhen . . . I should like to find that ruin."

Thurms turned to his friend. "So would I," he said meaningfully.

Kemheb grinned and held out his hand. "Comrades in arms, Thurms!"

They went down the dune together, with a breeze muttering at their backs, and a moony sand track ran on ahead of them like a hunting dog on a scent. They seemed to hear the night working around them as they walked, as though Aton were ushering blades of grass and buds of flowers and roots of saplings into the world with the touch of his hands

The Author

ROBERT EDMOND ALTER was less than sixteen when he knew he wanted to be an author. But when he left home at sixteen, he was determined to become a social worker. He became, instead, a citrus picker, a Hollywood extra, and for a short while a soldier. Finally, in his early thirties, he resumed his first ambition of becoming a writer. His score so far includes stories in major magazines, and four novels for young people.

Bob Alter lives with his wife and teen-age daughter in Altadena, California.

www.ingramcontent.com/pod-product-compliance
Lightning Source LLC
LaVergne TN
LVHW091254080426
835510LV00007B/259